Foreword by *New York Times* Bestselling Author

C H R I S   B R A D Y

WAVEMAKERS

HOW SMALL ACTS OF COURAGE CAN CHANGE THE WORLD

LIFE Leadership Essentials Series

First Edition, May 2014
10 9 8 7 6 5 4 3 2 1

Published by:

Obstaclés Press
4072 Market Place Dr.
Flint, MI 48507

Scripture quotations marked "KJV" are taken from the Holy Bible, King James Version, Cambridge, 1769.

Scripture quotations marked "NASB" are taken from the New American Standard Bible®, Copyright © 1960, 1962, 1963, 1968, 1971, 1972, 1973, 1975, 1977, 1995 by The Lockman Foundation. Used by permission. (www.Lockman.org)

lifeleadership.com

ISBN 978-0-9913474-7-6

Cover design and layout by Norm Williams, nwa-inc.com

Printed in the United States of America

CONTENTS

FOREWORD

by Chris Brady

The crowd was larger than usual for such an event, and it soon became evident that the venue would be packed. The amount of people who had turned out that day was indeed noteworthy, but even more so was the makeup of that crowd. For in those balcony seats sat a virtual "Who's Who" of London high society. There were noblemen and ladies, Members of Parliament, other elected officials, and ambassadors. There were dignitaries and policy makers. And there were even a few, precious few, friends of the man who was standing alone at the metal gate in the center of the room.

The assembly was being held in Whitehall Palace in an octagonal room nicknamed the "Cockpit." The attraction was the interrogation of a colonial representative who had shared with the public a private letter from a colonial Governor. This had caught everyone by surprise: the colonists because it confirmed for them the second-class treatment they felt they were receiving from the Crown; the members of the British government because it confirmed their suspicions that this particular representative was aligned with the rebels; the representative himself because this incident, for the first time, shed light on the true depth of the brewing conflict between crown and colony. In fact, for this particular colonial representative, it would be a wakeup call that would rouse him from his slumber and forge a fire of determination that wouldn't burn out until complete independence had been established.

The year was 1774, and on that late January day, Benjamin Franklin would be confronted with a truth he had somehow been slow to realize: that the colonies should never be reconciled to their subservient role under the British government. Up to that day, he had held to the notion that the rift could be repaired and that the colonies were better off remaining British subjects.

At first, the meeting was a minor irritant to Franklin. He had done nothing morally or legally wrong, and at most, he could be accused of behaving contrary to aristocratic etiquette. But as the vicious Solicitor General Alexander Wedderburn, known far and wide for his vitriol, took his usual rancor to new heights, Franklin grew angrier and angrier. It is said that by the end of the extended diatribe, in which Franklin was accused of all manner of treachery and treason, Franklin's hands gripped the metal railing on the "bar" so firmly that it appeared he could rip it from the floor. Throughout, however, his countenance was stoic as a Greek statue. Finding himself in a situation utterly ridiculous, by sheer force of will, he remained silent.

Soon thereafter, Franklin sailed back to North America from England, never to return. What had become a happy home for him, replete with fame and notoriety, friendships with the highest scientific minds of the time, membership in the distinguished Royal Society of the Arts, and stimulation for his abundantly curious mind, had now become enemy territory. He would thereafter throw himself enthusiastically into the cause of freedom for the colonies, accepting the role of Ambassador to France, where he would masterfully secure the money, guns, ships, and support of King Louis XVI that would all prove so crucial in the winning of the War of Independence.

The disturbance that began in the "Cockpit" had grown into a mighty wave that ultimately swamped an empire. And while one man didn't do it all alone, it couldn't have happened without what that one man alone did.

This type of occurrence, in which a single event triggers massive passion within the breast of an individual that results in a title wave of change is so enthralling, so thrilling, as to keep us talking about it hundreds of years later. In a world where most people seem intent on not "rocking the boat," it is infinitely interesting (and instructive) when someone not only rocks the boat but intentionally makes waves. We watch those waves crash up onto the rocky shores of the status quo and wash it out to sea, leaving a world behind in the wash that is forever transformed.

What's more, these are not rare events. Look through the pages of history, and there, everywhere, are people who have, in large ways and small, been inspired to stir up waves of change. Look around you in our modern world, and again there, everywhere, are more examples.

In this book, we call them "Wavemakers." They are that particular slice of humanity that cannot stand to leave things the way they found them. They seem to understand that to make a difference, they have to be different. And importantly, they realize that the opinions of those who do *not* care to make a difference don't matter to them. Whereas most people seem to go through life merely trying to survive, seeking short-term gratifications and a sample of life's pleasures, there are a select few who are utterly discontent with the status quo. These extraordinary few can't take things as they find them and can't leave things alone. They are driven by a desire to remake the world into something more in line with their own unique vision of how it should be. And in so doing, they create waves of change that roll through the pages of time.

We study several representative cases of this type of person in this book. They come from all walks of life, persuasions, and political affiliations. But they have one thing in common: a life dedicated to making waves. Some call them heroes; some villains. But no one can ignore them. And since they cannot be ignored, they may as well be studied. Through such study, we will not only be mightily entertained but hugely instructed. And perhaps, just maybe, we will be inspired to make waves of our own!

Chris Brady
New York Times Bestselling Author
Cofounder, CEO, and Creative Director of LIFE Leadership

THE POWER OF THE RIPPLE EFFECT

*A ship in harbor is safe, but that is
not what ships are built for.*

—JOHN A. SHEDD

On this vast and tumultuous ocean we call life, most people fear the waves and are content to lounge in safe harbors. They may avoid a few storms, but they also never experience the full joy that only adventurers feel or reap the rewards gained by intrepid voyagers.

There are others—very few—who not only brave the waves, but also make them. These courageous Wavemakers are not content to sit on the beach and watch the tide. They yearn to be out on the open ocean, leading change, attacking the status quo.

Wavemakers understand the power of the ripple effect. They never underestimate their small and seemingly insignificant actions because they know they can lead to dramatic results in the future. Wavemakers work tirelessly for years, ignored, unacknowledged, and often ridiculed, because their vision of a brighter future is stronger than their fear of embarrassment.

Wavemakers are generational thinkers. They consider the consequences of their actions for those who will follow behind them. They strive to make things better for future generations. As author Stephen Palmer wrote in his book, *Uncommon Sense: A Common Citizen's Guide to Rebuilding America*:

> It's far easier to go along with the crowd and never make waves than it is to take a stand, go against the grain of popular culture, and make a lasting difference.
>
> Martin Luther King, Jr. took the road less traveled and was murdered for it, as was Gandhi. George Washington, wanting nothing more than to be a quiet farmer, suffered through years of toil and hardship as a general, then stayed in the trenches during two terms as president. Joan of Arc was burned at the stake for attempting to free France from the rule of England and claiming that she saw visions. Corrie ten Boom endured the horrors of Nazi concentration camps for hiding Jews. Jesus Christ was crucified for speaking truth.
>
> *The people who rock the status quo boat are usually kicked off the boat and are often drowned. But because of their courage and sacrifice, the rest of us enjoy smooth sailing.*[1]

Such Wavemakers derive their strength not only from deep within themselves, but also from God, to whom they give their full allegiance. They thirst not for praise of man, but for validation from their Father. They can endure the mocking of earthly crowds because they're uplifted by heavenly hosts. They can withstand years of thankless, anonymous struggle in obscure trenches because they know they're laying in store treasures in heaven.

Wavemakers know who they are and the purpose for which they were born. But that clarity doesn't come automatically or by accident. Wavemakers seek it consciously and passionately.

Author Roy H. Williams once shared at a seminar the following insight, which he learned from Mike Metzger, the president of the Clapham Institute:

> You meet four kinds of people on the ocean of life.
>
> Those who **drift** just go with the flow. The wind and the waves control their speed and direction. The drifter quietly floats along and says, "Whatever."
>
> Those who **surf** are always riding a wave, the next big thing. They stay excited until the wave fades away, then they scan the horizon for something new. Surfers don't usually get anywhere, but they make a lot of noise and put on a good show.
>
> Those who **drown** seem to stay in the center of a storm. It doesn't matter how often you rescue them, they'll soon be in another crisis, crying, "Help me,

save me, it's been the worst week of my life. I don't know what I'm going to do."

Those who **sail** are navigating toward a fixed point. They counteract the wind and waves by adjusting the rudder and shifting the sails to stay on course.

But without an immovable, fixed point in your life, there can be no sailing. There's nothing for you but drift, surf, or drown.[2]

Wavemakers have a fixed point, a North Star that provides their standard, drives all their actions, and gives them meaning. They know *exactly* what they're trying to make happen and how they define success.

In this book, you'll learn the stories of seven Wavemakers whose ripples have resounded through history. You'll accompany them on their voyages, from their humble beginnings to their illustrious ends. You'll witness their defeats, share their triumphs, and take notes from their mistakes.

And through the process, you'll learn how you can become a Wavemaker yourself. You'll be inspired to do more than wait for waves to surf and instead to make waves with the wake of your impact. You'll realize the importance of all your choices, no matter how insignificant they may seem in the moment. You'll learn to consider the consequences of your actions on other people and on future generations.

Someone once said, "If you ain't making waves, you ain't kickin' hard enough." This book will teach you how to kick hard and effectively so you can make the right waves that create a big, positive difference over time.

DISCLAIMER: Please do not mistake our featuring specific "Wavemakers" in this book as an endorsement of all their beliefs, strategies, and practices. The purpose of this book is not to highlight people we necessarily agree with on every point, but rather to showcase leaders who have been effective at enacting broad and fundamental change. You may disagree on many points with any or all featured Wavemakers. But don't let your disagreements keep you from learning from these leaders how to make a difference.

CHAPTER ONE

FORTUNE'S WHEEL

Be like the cliff against which the waves continually break;
but it stands firm and tames the fury of the water around it.

—MARCUS AURELIUS

Crowds of tribesmen gathered on the hills overlooking the little town and harbor in northern Israel, anxiously watching the fierce and bloody battle that would determine their fate.

On the harbor side, the defending captain, after observing the crowds in the hills, wrote, "'Tis on the issue of this conflict that depends the opinion of the multitude of the spectators on the surrounding hills, who wait only to see how it ends to join the victor....Constantinople, and even Vienna, must feel the shock."[1] As much as he understood the import of his actions, he vastly underestimated the scale of the historic decision determined by that battle.

On the inland side, the attacking general mused, "This wretched place has cost me a number of men and wasted much time. But things are too far advanced not to attempt a last effort. If I succeed, I shall march upon Damascus and Aleppo. I shall overturn the Turkish Empire and found in the east a new and grand empire that will fix my place in the records of posterity."[2]

The tribesmen did not have to wait long for the unlikely outcome. The general did, indeed, fix his place in the records of history. But it wasn't for the empire he lusted for, which eluded his grasp largely because of this one portentous battle. Later in his life, reflecting on this battle, the French general wrote of the British captain, *"Cet homme m'a fait manquer ma fortune"* ("That man made me miss my destiny").[3] Those observing tribesmen were not the only ones affected by the outcome of that battle. The history of the world changed, and the fates of millions of people were forever altered because that captain, Sir Sidney Smith, stood firm against the sweeping tyranny of Napoleon Bonaparte in the consequential battle for Acre, Israel, in March 1799.

Born on June 21, 1764, into a military and naval family on the "fringes of fashionable society and political power,"[4] William Sidney Smith was an energetic young boy. As a child, he was described as a "most vivacious specimen of juvenility—quick, daring and mercurial and not far removed from a little Pickle."[5] (We assume that a "pickle" is what we would call a "Rascal," based on Chris Brady's book *Rascal: Making a Difference by Becoming an Original Character*.[6]) That temperament characterized his life.

At the age of eleven, he displayed his natural resourcefulness that would serve him well throughout his naval career. One summer evening, Sidney did not show up for evening prayers. A frantic search ensued. He was found in the middle of the nearby lake, sitting with a little girl in a washtub. He had taken her out for a joyride, only to lose the long pole he had used to push the washtub from shore. They were in deep water, and no other boat was available to rescue them. The adults brainstormed but were stumped as to how to rescue the stranded youth. Then little Sidney offered a suggestion. He told them to take his kite string and tie it to his favorite dog. He called the dog, and it swam out to him. The adults then used the kite string to lug them into shore. Just as his father was about to scold him, the boy calmly said, "Now, Father, we will go to prayers."

"We had better," his father responded in exasperation.[7]

After attending the elite Tonbridge School for boys in Kent, England, and receiving a classical education, Sidney followed his father's career path and joined the Royal Navy in 1777, just before his thirteenth birthday. He was described at the time as small but "eminently handsome with clustering and curling black hair, dark, clear complexion and with a high colour....He evinced an utter contempt of danger and a decision of character that, under proper training, warranted the most sanguine hopes of future excellence."[8]

He spent the next seven years serving on various ships and seeing action in the American Revolutionary War, including an aborted attempt to relieve General Cornwallis in the besieged Yorktown. After displaying bravery in a scrape with a Spanish convoy off Cape St. Vincent, Sidney was appointed as a lieutenant on September 25, 1780, despite being under the required age of nineteen.

After Britain, France, and Spain signed a peace treaty in Versailles in 1783 recognizing the independence of the United States of America, Sidney was sent ashore and put on half-pay. Most sailors used their downtime to play and pursue other interests. But Sidney knew his purpose and was focused on a military career. Rather than sit around waiting to be told what to do, he searched for opportunities to improve his skills and usefulness to the navy. He chose to move to Normandy to learn French, thus "further qualifying [himself] for [his] country's service," as he put it.[9]

WAVEMAKER WISDOM

Don't wait for a boss or authority figure to tell you what to do. Look around and see what needs to be done. Find ways to enhance your usefulness and create value for others. Start a new project. Acquire a new skill. Read books and take courses to increase your knowledge in your industry. Wavemakers take initiative!

What's the best thing you can do right now to become more useful and valuable in the pursuit of your purpose?

While on leave learning French, ever vigilant in serving his country, he also engaged in overt espionage. After making friends with the governor of Normandy, he learned of a naval base being built nearby. He traveled to the location, watched the building activities, and reported them to the Board of Admiralty in London. His espionage proved to be addictive for him, as it added adventure to his tourism and, of course, increased his chances of promotion. But since Britain and France were at peace, he had little opportunity in either country to make himself useful.

His sights turned to the Mediterranean, particularly along the North African coast, where piracy at sea and slavery ashore continued to threaten European trading nations. The sultan of Morocco had been threatening his neighbors to the north. In 1787, suspecting that war would break out, Smith set out on a tour to learn the coasts, harbors, and military forces of Morocco.

He detailed his findings in a letter to the Secretary of the Admiralty, warning him that the Royal Navy was unprepared to guard against the threat to shipping on both sides of the Strait of Gibraltar. He urged the secretary to form a second squadron and then got to the point:

> I am therefore on my return to England in the earnest hope that their Lordships will enable me to employ it to advantage in the protection of our trade by giving me command of a force adequate to the destruction of his naval force, even in his harbours....I hope their Lordships will not consider this my inferiority of rank as an obstacle to grant

me the honour I request but rather trust that what I want in professional experience and ability will be made up by local knowledge and zeal for the public service."[10]

Fortunately, the threat of war subsided, and his services were not needed. However, his proactive letter caught the eye of the Board of Admiralty, and his name was noted.

WAVEMAKER WISDOM

Be a problem solver, not just a problem pointer. When you notice flaws, mistakes, or weaknesses, don't just point them out; offer detailed solutions with your observations. Be proactive in seeking out potential issues and creating solutions. And don't let your age or lack of experience stop you from making positive suggestions! Even if your recommendations aren't applied immediately, you'll at least catch people's attention and become known as a go-getter.

What is the greatest problem your company, business, team, or family faces right now? What solution might you offer? And how might you put yourself forward to enact it?

Once again, Smith found himself looking for an opportunity to deepen his military experience. One path was to apply to the admiralty for a long leave and then become a mercenary for a nation that was at war but not in conflict with British interests. Accordingly, in January 1790, he traveled to Copenhagen to assess his prospects of joining up with the Swedes in their conflict with Russia. The Swedish monarch, King Gustavus, was quite taken with Smith. "The great reputation you have acquired in serving your own country with equal success and valour," he told Smith, "and the profound calm which England enjoys not affording you any opportunity to display your talents at present, induce me to propose to you to enter into my service."[11]

Champing at the bit for action, Smith returned to London to ask permission to fight with the Swedes on a temporary commission. When his superiors were agonizingly slow to respond, he made a self-serving assumption that he would eventually receive permission and offered his services to King Gustavus. The king promptly gave Smith command of his light forces, consisting of three small frigates, five square-rigged bomb ketches, and twenty galleys, all manned by four thousand marines, along with seventy-two gunboats, each mounted with twenty-four-pound guns in bow and stern and rowed by seventy men.

In July, after several skirmishes with the Russians, Smith engaged in his greatest battle to date. Heading into battle, King Gustavus was filled with apprehension; in fact, fully expecting to be beaten, he had drafted his own capitulation prior to the battle. As galleys and gunboats fought oar to oar, Smith's training of his crews shone through the smoke and confusion. At the end of a long, frantic night, the Russians had lost sixty-four ships and nearly a thousand men, and the Swedes had taken more than six thousand prisoners. Under Smith's leadership, the Swedes had lost only four ships and a few men. For his courage and skill in battle, King Gustavus awarded Smith with a Swedish knighthood, thus giving him the "Sir" that he would use throughout his life (although many British officers mocked him for doing so).

Having proved himself in battle and demonstrated skill as an intelligence officer, Smith was commissioned to serve in the Turkish Navy and to take the opportunity of "examining the Black Sea, Bosphorous, Sea of Marmora, Dardanelles, Archipelago, and Ionian Islands,"[12] in a similar fashion to his investigation in Morocco. Thus, when France's King Louis was executed in January of 1793, sparking the French Revolution, and France subsequently declared war on Britain, Smith heard the news in Smyrna. "This intelligence was to him like the sound of the trumpet to a war horse," a friend wrote.[13]

Smith was anxious to return to England to offer his services. Nevertheless, he was not one to pass up a leadership opportunity. He rounded up several dozen unemployed British seamen who were loafing on the waterfront and recruited them with the promise of a passage home. He purchased a ship with his own money and set sail with a crew of forty men.

WAVEMAKER WISDOM

It's not enough to be a stand-alone maverick; you must actively recruit people to your cause. Being a Wavemaker isn't about lone-wolf, cantankerous protesting. It's about genuine leadership, creating a following, making a real difference.

What people do you know in your life who are waiting for a cause to rally behind? How can you recruit them to your cause?

Smith was sent to Toulon, a Mediterranean port town on the southern tip of France, to assist Lord Hood, who had been invited by French royalists to help defend it against advancing republicans. Although the naval base there was situated well for defense, Hood was short on troops. His force, consisting of British sailors and marines, Spanish troops, and a few other allies, amounted to only 17,000 men, which was not enough to defend the perimeter. A French republican army more than twice that size—its soldiers intoxicated with revolutionary zeal—arrived and attacked with ferocity.

Smith sailed into the port just as the defenses were about to collapse. Unknown to Hood and Smith, a "stocky, sallow, and taciturn" Corsican was in the ranks of the French armies, serving as a colonel of artillery: Napoleon Bonaparte. This would be the first time Smith and Napoleon would face each other in battle. And neither one would forget the other. Napoleon's genius supplied the strategy that brought Toulon to its knees, but, in parting, Smith's innovative tenacity would strike a crushing blow to the French naval fleet.

Napoleon wrote of the battle:

> It was I who proposed the plan of attack that resulted in the reduction of Toulon. I regarded all the proposals [of the convention] as totally useless and was of the opinion that a regular siege was simply not necessary. If from fifteen to twenty mortars, thirty or forty pieces of cannon and furnaces for red-hot balls could be positioned where they could maintain fire upon every point of the greater and lesser road-steads, then it was evident that the combined [allied] squadron would be obliged to withdraw....That being so, I was convinced that the combined forces would prefer to withdraw the garrison.[14]

Napoleon was right, and using his strategy, he captured the commanding headland. It was now just a matter of time before Toulon would fall, forcing the allied troops to evacuate and the naval fleet to withdraw. Through the battle, Smith, currently holding no appointment in the Royal Navy, essentially sat frustrated on the sidelines. He wasted no time sulking, however, and surveyed the situation, eager to find some way to be of service. As Toulon was the principal French naval base in the Mediterranean, he took careful note of the French warships in the dockyards—a total of fifty-eight ships, including thirty-two of the line and fourteen frigates.

A final council of war was held by the admiral with the Spanish admiral and the commanders of the land forces. Some of the British naval captains were irritated that Smith, an unemployed officer on half-pay, should attend. Smith pointed out that while they commanded troops who were paid *for* them, he had paid for his own crew.

During the council, Smith asked, "What do you mean to do with all those fine ships of the enemy? Do you mean to leave them behind?"

"What do you propose to do with them?" Hood replied.

"Burn them to be sure," Smith declared.

Smith later wrote, "I volunteered it under the disadvantage of there being no previous preparation for it whatever."[15]

Hood agreed and gave Smith the command of a flotilla of gunboats and two Royal Navy captains, fourteen lieutenants, seven midshipmen, and a surgeon to carry out the plan, ordering, "You must burn every French ship you possibly can."[16] In a reconciliatory effort, Hood also told him to ask the Spanish admiral, Don Langara, for help. Smith boarded the Spanish flagship, the *Concepción*, and asked the admiral to use his gunboats. He later noted that "they were reluctantly granted me and as reluctantly followed me."[17] Given the reluctance of his Spanish colleagues, Smith was apprehensive of the outcome. His apprehension proved to be justified.

His flotilla set sail. Before they reached the shore, all but one Spanish boat had disappeared. In addition to that solitary ship, he was left with his own ship, the *Swallow*; three British gunboats; a mortar-boat without ammunition; and another small boat. The demolition parties landed and began placing combustibles and fuses in the storehouses and ships. Ascertaining their intentions, French republicans began raining fire on them. Smith later wrote:

> A great multitude of the enemy continued to draw down the hill towards the dockyard wall and, as night closed in, they came near enough to pour in an irregular though quick fire on us...from the heights which overlook it. We kept them at bay by discharges of grape-shot from time to time, which prevented their coming so near as to discover the insufficiency of our force to repel a closer attack.[18]

While the demolition parties worked, a fireship, the *Vulcan*, was placed into position broadside to the moored French warships. The enemy began beating on the dockyard gates while the British officers anxiously looked at their watches, awaiting the signal to fire. When it came, they were satisfied to see that they had done their work well, as a number of the French ships exploded and burned.

The plan was not executed flawlessly, however. A flash ignited prematurely on the *Vulcan*, and the ship erupted in flames. Furthermore, Smith's hunch about the Spaniards was realized. The French revolutionary Robespierre later wrote:

> The Spaniards...fled on all sides...and left the English everywhere to bite the dust....The ships

which the Spaniards had to burn, they did not set fire to....Conformably to the agreement, the Spaniards were to attempt the destruction of some others, by cutting the cables, and by blowing up some old French men-of-war, laden with powder, in the harbour. This, indeed, they did, but too late to cause any damage."

Napoleon himself wrote, "Sir Sidney Smith set them on fire, and they would have all been burned if the Spaniards had behaved well. It was the prettiest *feu d'artifice* [fireworks] possible."[19]

Nevertheless, the venture exacted a heavy price on the French Navy. Smith concluded:

Having now set fire to everything within our reach, exhausted our combustible preparations, and our strengths, to such a degree that the men absolutely dropped on the oars, we directed our course to join the fleet, running the gauntlet under a few ill-directed shots from the forts...now occupied by the enemy...we proceeded to the place appointed for the embarkation of troops and took off as many as we could."[20]

Smith and his men had burned or sunk ten ships of the line, two frigates, and two corvettes. Most of the other surviving ships were those that the Spanish had been charged with burning.

Historian and biographer Tom Pocock wrote, "By any standards, Smith's achievement had been remarkable. He had destroyed what amounted to an entire battle-fleet, more than had been achieved in any action at sea that had won the victorious admiral honours and wealth."[21]

As all leaders experience, not everyone appreciated Smith's exploits. In fact, he was criticized soundly for being too self-confident and going over the heads of his immediate superiors, among other things. Smith was certainly not the most humble of leaders, but much of the resentment could be attributed to petty jealousy.

Smith returned to London on January 15, 1794, to find that the admiralty was satisfied with his feat and that the public lauded him as the first hero of the new war. After a few months' delay in finding him a new appointment, he was given the command of the thirty-eight-gun frigate *Diamond*. He was also gratified when Lord Spencer asked Smith to transport him to Flushing on his way to Vienna.

While they were en route, a few French batteries on the southern shore fired shots at the frigate, which fell short. Smith immediately launched into explaining to Lord Spencer a scheme he had been working on for several years. Having experienced their use in the Baltic years earlier, Smith saw the need for powerful gunboats that could be manned in shallow waters in similar situations. Upon their arrival at Flushing, Lord Spencer wrote to the Secretary State of War, William Windham:

> I promised Sir Sidney Smith to write to you something about what he calls his ideas but my own ideas have really been so turned and twisted and tumbled about ever since that I protest I have been pretty nearly shaken out of my head. In general,

however, I remember he said a good deal about the French coasting ships, which, by their being very flat bottomed, can run into shoal water where none of our ships can follow them, and, of course, he is very desirous of having a fleet of flat-bottomed vessels at his command….He is certainly an odd, eccentric man but he is very clever and has a great deal of contrivance about him and if he could somehow be put into activity without giving offence to the more regular and orderly sort of Geniuses, who I believe all look upon him as a fellow of the College of Physicians does upon a Quack doctor, he might be of great service.[22]

WAVEMAKER WISDOM

Never, ever stop innovating. When there's no path, make a path. Use your imagination and creativity to find ways you can be of service. Your innovation is not limited to your title, position, or status; it's only limited by the constraints you place on yourself. When you identify ways to innovate and create value, move forward with faith and confidence—even and *especially* when it's never been tried before. Initiative is priceless.

Yes, you will be criticized. Expect opposition. Remember Teddy Roosevelt's counsel:

It is not the critic who counts: not the man who points out how the strong man stumbles or where the doer of deeds could have done better. The credit belongs to the man who is actually in the arena, whose face is marred by dust and sweat and blood, who strives valiantly, who errs and comes up short again and again, because there is no effort without error or shortcoming, but who knows the great enthusiasms, the great devotions, who spends himself for a worthy cause; who, at the best, knows, in the end, the triumph of high achievement, and who, at the worst, if he fails, at least he fails while daring greatly, so that his place shall never be with those cold and timid souls who knew neither victory nor defeat.

Where can you innovate in your business or career? What can you do that's never been done before? What's your detailed plan for executing it? What's holding you back?

After two years of battling the French Navy, on April 18, 1796, Sir Sydney steered the *Diamond* into the port of Le Havre at the mouth of the Seine River on the northeastern shore of France. His target was the *Vengeur*, a privateer lugger, which had preyed upon British shipping in the English Channel. Under cover of night, Smith took a crew of thirty-three men armed with swords, cutlasses, pikes, pistols, and tomahawks in small boats and pulled alongside the *Vengeur*. They sprang aboard, and after fierce hand-to-hand fighting, the French surrendered and were taken below the hatch.

It was discovered that one of the Frenchmen had cut the anchor cable and the lugger was drifting. The British put up the sails. But the wind had dropped, and the ship began drifting into the Seine. With no wind, Smith's other men aboard the *Diamond* could only watch helplessly. At daybreak, the lugger was spotted by men aboard a French corvette, and an alarm was sounded. Smith sent his prisoners ashore and prepared to fight.

French boats encircled the British. The fighting was frantic but brief, and Smith knew it was only a matter of time before they would be captured. He wrote:

> My brave fellows collected round me, on the enemy's closing on us, swearing to die fighting by me....The servants behaved admirably and the boys acted like men....The enemy prepared to board us, sword in hand, refusing us quarter with insults and imprecations. Our firm posture checked them and my harangue to their chief relented their fury and turned their resentment into admiration. It was acknowledged that we could not get away and that further resistance would not avail but we were determined to die with arms in our hands if they would not give us quarter and this determination saved us.

Smith surrendered his sword to the French captain, and he and his men were taken captive.

Smith was not unduly concerned; the standard protocol was to exchange prisoners of war, and he fully expected to be once again commanding a ship soon. But incensed over his devastating incendiary exploits in Toulon, the French kept him prisoner under a technicality: since he was on half-pay with no official commission during the Toulon campaign, they labeled him a spy and arsonist, thus avoiding the standard prisoner-of-war procedures.

As biographer Edward Howard wrote:

> His justly deserved fame: his unceasing vigilance, and his courage bordering on rashness, had rendered him peculiarly obnoxious to the revolutionized nation, and the French Directors showed the respect they felt for his heroism by departing from the established system, consecrated by the law of nations, which humanely prescribes an exchange of prisoners during the continuance of war. Captain Sir Sidney Smith was not to be exchanged. He was conveyed to Paris, and confined in the Temple [prison] for the space of two years—a time truly dreadful when spent in rigid incarceration.

Smith realized the danger of his predicament when the French Directory charged him with attempting to set fire to the town and docks of Le Havre. It was a spurious claim, the only evidence being sulfur that French sailors had discovered aboard the captured *Vengeur*. Still, it could lead to a death warrant for Smith.

With nothing to do but wait, Smith began writing letters to both French and British authorities and devising other schemes to escape. During his stay, he developed a cordial and interesting relationship with his jailkeeper. One day, while dining with Smith, the jailer noticed him looking wistfully out a window. This concerned the jailer, since the window opened onto the street. Smith, laughing, said, "I know what you are thinking of; but fear not. It is now three o'clock. I will make a truce with you till midnight; and I give you my word of honour, until that time, even were the doors open, I would not escape. When that hour is passed, my promise is at an end, and we are enemies again."

"Sir," the jailer replied, "your word is a safer bond thatnmy bars or bolts: till midnight, therefore, I am perfectly easy."[23]

WAVEMAKER WISDOM

Nothing opens the doors to influence like integrity. Make your word your bond. Without fail, do what you say you will do. As Karl G. Maeser said:

I have been asked what I mean by "word of honor." I will tell you. Place me behind prison walls—walls of stone ever so high, ever so thick, reaching ever so far into the ground—there is a possibility that in some way or another I might be

I have been askable to escape; but stand me on the floor and draw a chalk line around me and have me give my word of honor never to cross it. Can I get out of that circle? No, never! I'd die first.

Are you living with integrity? Is there a relationship you need to repair because you have not kept your word? Has your integrity ever earned the respect of your enemies?

On December 5, 1797, from their prison cells Smith and his companions heard sounds of gunfire. They were told it was the firing of salutes to welcome General Bonaparte home from his victorious campaign in Italy. Thinking he might feel chivalrous toward an old adversary, Smith wrote a letter to Bonaparte asking him to persuade the Directory to designate him as a prisoner of war. But Bonaparte refused to even receive the letter.

Smith proceeded to write another letter on the wooden shutter of his cell window, hoping it would eventually reach the ears of Bonaparte. He wrote in French:

One has to admit that Fortune's wheel makes strange revolutions but, before it can be truly called a revolution, the turn of the wheel must be complete. Today you are as high as you can be but I do not envy you your happiness because I have a still greater happiness and that is to be as low in Fortune's wheel as I can go, so that as soon as that capricious lady turns her wheel again, I shall rise for the same reason that you will fall.

I do not write this to distress you but to bring you the same consolation that I have when you reach the point where I am. You will occupy this same prison—why not you as well as I? I did not expect to be shut up here, any more than you do now.

In a partisan war it is a crime in the eyes of one's opponents to do one's duty honourably as you do today, and, in consequence, you embitter your enemies against you. No doubt you will reply, "I do not fear the hatred I arouse in them. Has not the voice of the people declared for me?" That is well spoken. Sleep in peace. Before six months have passed, if not today, you will learn what the reward is for serving such masters, the reward for all the good you have done them. Pausanias wrote long ago, "He who has placed all his hopes on the friendship of the public has never come to a happy end."

But, of course, I do not have to convince you that you will come here because to read these lines you must be here. I assume that you will have this room also because the gaoler is a good man: he gave me the best room and will do as much for you.[24]

WAVEMAKER WISDOM

Keep your chin up during trials. The age-old wisdom "This, too, shall pass" really is true! "Fortune's wheel" will turn. When you look back on your trials, you will be grateful for all they taught you. So act admirably through them so you will be proud of your conduct when you look back on it.

What is the hardest thing you have had to endure in your life? What lessons did you learn from it?

Indeed, the letter did make its way into French newspapers and Napoleon undoubtedly read it. We can assume the tormenting effect it had on his mind while in exile until his death.

Despite Smith's defiance, his prospects seemed bleaker than ever. He was left to assume that the British government had abandoned its attempts to negotiate his release. After almost two years of mind-numbing imprisonment, Smith was more determined than ever to escape. However, it was not his own ingenuity but rather the help of French royalists that presented the opportunity.

On February 24, 1798, a group of disguised royalists arrived at the prison and presented the keeper with official papers for transporting Smith and his men to a different prison. They were released, and the royalists brought them to Le Havre, where they boarded an open fishing boat and were picked up on May 5 by an English ship. They arrived in London on May 8.

Fortune's wheel had turned for Smith, and his return to battle would soon turn the wheel of fortune to Napoleon's demise. In fact, Bonaparte's military secretary, Fauvelet de Bourrienne, penned these ominous words when he heard the news: "Such a seemingly ordinary escape, yet one that was to wreck the most gigantic projects and the most audacious plans."[25]

Two days later, while Smith was hailed as a hero in London, Bonaparte sailed for Egypt, intent on eastern conquest. Napoleon's strategy was to occupy Egypt with three goals: "To establish on the Nile a French colony, which would prosper without slaves and serve France in place of the republic of Santo Domingo and all the sugar islands; to open a market for our manufactures in Africa, Arabia, and Syria, and supply our commerce with all the production of those vast countries."[26] His limitless imagination conjured fantasies of colonization:

> What could be made of that beautiful country in fifty years of prosperity and good government? One's imagination delights in the enchanting vistas. A thousand irrigation sluices would tame and distribute the overflow of the Nile over every part of the territory....Numerous immigrants from deepest Africa, from Arabia, from Syria, from Greece, from France, from Italy, from Poland, from Germany, would quadruple the population. Trade with India would again flow through its ancient route....France, being mistress of Egypt, would also regain mastery over Hindustan.[27]

Aside from these commercial aspirations, Napoleon revealed his true intentions when he wrote, "The day is not far off when we shall appreciate the necessity, in order to really destroy England, to seize Egypt." The ultimate goal was to use the Egyptian conquest to overthrow England's commercial stronghold in India. "To go to Egypt," he boasted, "to establish myself there and found a French colony will require some months, but as soon as I have made England tremble for the safety of India, I shall return to Paris and give the enemy its death-blow."[28]

These grandiose intentions, however, were still unknown in London. The admiralty, trying to prepare for any contingency, decided that a squadron of warships must be sent into the Mediterranean on armed reconnaissance. Because of his previous experience with fighting the Russians and serving in the Turkish Navy, Sir Sidney Smith was the obvious man to lead the fleet. As Lord Grenville wrote to the First Lord of the Admiralty, "The officer to command such a squadron should be Sir Sidney Smith, not of our partiality for him, but thinking that his name is better known to both Russians and Turks, and his character better suited to act with them than many of the other officers."[29]

WAVEMAKER WISDOM

Prepare for the future by constantly seeking to increase your knowledge, add to your skill set, and forge new relationships. You never know what you'll be led to in the future by the skills and attributes you develop today.

In his book, *Rich Dad, Poor Dad*, Robert Kiyosaki teaches, "When you're young, work to learn rather than to earn."[30] Choose jobs and career opportunities not for their earning potential but rather for their personal development potential. Read a wide variety of books outside your field of expertise. Attend seminars that may not seem to apply to you today but do hold long-term potential.

What should you be doing today to gain more knowledge and broaden your skill set for future endeavors?

As captain of the HMS *Tigre*, an eighty-gun ship of the line, Sir Sydney arrived in Constantinople on December 26, 1798, with the mission to strengthen Turkish opposition to Napoleon and to assist the Turks in destroying the French Army.

Napoleon had defeated Ottoman forces in Egypt, imposing military and civil law in Cairo, and then marched along the Mediterranean coast with 13,000 troops through the Ottoman province of Syria (which included modern-day Israel, Palestine, Syria, and Lebanon). He captured Gaza and Jaffa with little restraint in his brutality and massacred thousands of Turkish soldiers. He then marched with his army to Acre, a small port town of 15,000 citizens in modern-day Israel.

Having ascertained their route, Smith sailed to Acre and arrived before Napoleon on March 21, 1799. He and his troops began helping the Turkish commander, Jezzar Pasha, to reinforce the defenses and old walls surrounding the city. He also supplied the Turks with cannons and soldiers.

As the battle neared, both Smith and Bonaparte understood how critical Acre was strategically. As long as the British controlled the sea, the French could not bypass the city and continue their conquest because the British and their allies could land an army there behind the French Army. Acre, with its crumbling walls, and Sir Sidney Smith, with his solid determination, were all that stood between Napoleon and his ambition. Yet Napoleon was confident, for his army outnumbered the defenders three to one, and the walls of Acre were no match for siege guns.

On March 26, Bonaparte watched from a hill while his batteries opened fire on the city, fully expecting to win the battle within days. But he had underestimated Acre's defenses and Smith's resolve. French assaults were driven back repeatedly, and the defenders prevented several attempts to mine the walls. Using his control of the sea, Smith captured the French siege artillery, which had been shipped from Egypt. He also denied the French Army the use of the coastal road from Jaffa by bombarding troops from the sea. It soon became apparent that this would be a long siege, and Napoleon became increasingly impatient.

It wasn't until early May that replacement French siege artillery arrived overland. Subsequently, a breach was blown in the defenses. But once again, the assault was repelled. A French officer wrote:

It was clear that it was impossible to penetrate it. The enemy, installed at the top of the tower and hidden behind the battlements, flattened our troops with rocks, shells, and hand grenades. However, since nothing could turn back our troops, the Turks resorted to powder kegs which they threw on them. All our men were suffocated although a few managed to run away half-burned."[31]

Out of frustration, Bonaparte, a master of psychological warfare, began distributing leaflets in Arabic proclaiming himself the defender of Islam, in an attempt to draw Turkish troops to his side. He also issued a proclamation to the Christians that he was a successor to the Crusaders and a defender of the faith. Acquiring copies of both, Smith reprinted and distributed each to the opposite side, so that Muslims saw Napoleon as a Christian champion and Christians saw him as a Muslim. As a result, an Islamic leader forbade his men to fight for the French and joined with the British. Smith didn't stop there. He also printed leaflets offering free passage to France for any surrendering soldier and had bundles of them thrown into the French trenches. Having met his match, the conceited general was infuriated.

Throughout the siege, Smith managed his post ferociously and tirelessly, seeming to be everywhere at once, directing naval operations from the *Tigre*, inspecting the defenses within the city, observing French activities from the walls, even roaming outside the defenses. On one occasion, he crept forward from the walls with a small group of men, when one soldier sighted French sharpshooters. The soldier warned, "I see them lying down under the ridges of sand, Sir Sidney, and they will put a ball through you before you can say Jack Robinson."[32] Then they were sighted and ran back to safety behind the walls.

On the evening of May 8, the day before Napoleon's final assault, Smith wrote of seeing the crowds of tribesmen observing from nearby hills. That same evening, Napoleon cursed: "This wretched place has cost me a number of men and wasted much time." He dreamt of founding "a new and grand empire that [would fix his] place in the records of posterity."

The attack began at 3:00 a.m. The French rushed forward and burst through a breach in the lines. But the allied troops held firm, and the French vanguard was driven back. "Sir Sidney is pretty well occupied," wrote Smith's secretary, "particularly in the smoke, musketry and ditch fight, all of which is becoming a matter of course."[33]

After a furious battle, the French were defeated, and the battlefield gradually fell silent. Smith sat down and composed a gratifying letter to Bonaparte:

> This last word ought not to escape my mouth… but circumstances remind me to wish that you would reflect on the instability of human affairs. In fact, could you have thought that a poor prisoner in a cell of the Temple prison—that an unfortunate for whom you refused, for a single moment, to give yourself any concern…could you have thought, I say, that this same man would have become your antagonist and have compelled you in the midst of the sands of Syria to raise the siege of a miserable, almost defenceless town? Such events, you must admit, exceed all human calculations. Believe me, general, adopt sentiments more moderate; that a man will not be your enemy who shall tell you that Asia is not a theatre made for your glory. This letter is a little revenge that I give myself.

Bonaparte, stung and furious, with over a third of his original force dead or disabled, made preparations to withdraw his army to Egypt. This was his first defeat and would prove to be the most devastating to his dream of conquest. In 1805, he asserted:

[If I had] been able to take Acre [in 1799], I would have put on a turban, I would have made my soldiers wear big Turkish trousers, and I would have exposed them to battle only in case of extreme necessity. I would have made them into a Sacred Battalion—my Immortals. I would have finished the war against the Turks with Arabic, Greek, and Armenian troops. Instead of a battle in Moravia, I would have won a Battle of Issus, I would have made myself emperor of the East, and I would have returned to Paris by way of Constantinople.

In short, had Napoleon won the battle for Acre, eventually he might have conquered the British empire by taking over commerce in India.

The wheel of fortune had turned a complete revolution, and the course of history changed because of the brave actions of Sir Sidney Smith. The ripple effects of his campaign at Acre are incalculable. General Bonaparte went down in history as a murderous tyrant, Captain Smith as a Wavemaking hero.

CHAPTER TWO

"WRAPPED AND SWALLOWED UP IN GOD"

Be noble! And the nobleness that lies
In other men, sleeping, but never dead,
Will rise in majesty to meet thine own.

—JAMES RUSSELL LOWELL

In 1874, Richard L. Dugdale, businessman, sociologist, and member of the executive committee of the Prison Association of New York, was commissioned to inspect thirteen county jails in upstate New York. He was surprised to discover that forty-two criminals in six different prisons were related by blood or marriage.

Curious to connect the dots and explain the phenomenon, he self-funded a study of the family in question, which hailed from Ulster County, New York. He published his findings in 1877 in *The Jukes: A Study in Crime, Pauperism, Disease and Heredity.*[1]

To protect their anonymity, he dubbed the family "Jukes," from a verb meaning "to roost," referring to the habit of certain birds to roost where they land, rather than flying home. The implication was that the Jukes family was indolent and lazy and "did not provide themselves with comforts, did not work steadily," as educator and pastor Albert Winship put it.[2]

Dugdale traced the family to a certain "Max Jukes," born in about 1720 of Dutch stock, and studied 1,200 of Max's descendants. His study revealed that Max Jukes's descendants included:

- Seven murderers
- Sixty thieves
- Fifty "women of debauchery"
- 130 other convicts
- 310 paupers (more than one in four of Max's 1,200 known descendants), representing over 2,300 cumulative years lived in poorhouses
- 400 who were physically wrecked by indulgent living

He estimated that Max Jukes's descendants cost the state more than $1,250,000. Only twenty of the 1,200 learned a trade, and ten of those learned it in a state prison. Even they were not regularly employed. Three hundred of the 1,200—one in four—died in infancy from lack of good care and good conditions.[3]

Now contrast this appalling family history with that of Jonathan Edwards, the Puritan preacher who lived from 1703 to 1758, was widely acknowledged to be "America's most important and original philosophical theologian," and played a critical role in shaping the First Great Awakening in New England from 1733 to 1735. At the turn of the twentieth century, Albert Winship traced Edwards's descendants almost 150 years after his death. At the time, his descendants included:

- One US Vice President
- Three US Senators
- Three governors
- Three mayors
- Thirteen college presidents
- Thirty judges
- Sixty-five professors
- Eighty public office holders
- 100 lawyers
- 100 missionaries

Interestingly, one of Edwards's descendants presided over the New York Prison Commission, which oversaw Richard Dugdale's study of the Jukes family.

What was the difference between Max Jukes and Jonathan Edwards? Why would one man spawn a bunch of degenerates and another a small army of model productive citizens? What was so special about Jonathan Edwards that he would engender such a legacy?

Consider that he died at the age of fifty-six, and his widow died a few weeks after him, leaving behind six of their eleven children under the age of twenty, the youngest being only eight years old. These orphaned children had little monetary inheritance. Biographer Albert Winship wrote:

> If Jonathan Edwards did not leave a large finan-
> cial legacy, he did impart to his children an intellec-
> tual capacity and vigor, moral character, and devotion
> to training which have projected themselves through
> eight generations without losing the strength and
> force of their great ancestor. Of the three sons and
> eight daughters of Jonathan Edwards there was not
> one, nor a husband or wife of one, whose character
> and ability, whose purpose and achievement were
> not a credit to this godly man. Of the seventy-five
> grandchildren, with their husbands and wives, there
> was but one for whom an apology may be offered,
> and nearly every one was exceptionally strong in
> scholarship and moral force.[4]

To get a sense of the impact he made, consider the praise that was heaped upon Edwards by his peers:

> "From the days of Plato there has been no life
> of more simple and imposing grandeur than that of
> Jonathan Edwards." —*Westminster Review*
>
> "The greatest thinker that America has
> produced." —James McCosh, president of Princeton
> University
>
> "The most original and acute thinker yet
> produced in America." —Moses Coit Tyler, author
> and history professor

"A prince among preachers. In our day there is no man who comes within a thousand miles of him." —Lyman Beecher, Presbyterian minister and leader of the Second Great Awakening

"The most gifted man of the 18th Century, perhaps the most profound thinker in the world." —*Hollister's History of Connecticut*

"One of the acutest and most powerful of reasoners." —*Edinburgh Review*

"The greatest of theologians." —Dr. Thomas Chalmers, Scottish minister, professor of theology, political economist and leader of the Church of Scotland and of the Free Church of Scotland

"One of the greatest metaphysicians of his age." —*Encyclopaedia*

"His gigantic specimen of theological argument is as near to perfection as we may expect any human composition to approach. He unites the sharpness of the scimitar and the strength of the battle-axe." —*London Quarterly Review*

"*The Freedom of the Will* by Mr. Edwards is the greatest achievement of the human intellect. —Daniel Webster

"The first man of the world during the second quarter of the 18th Century." —*Griswold's Prose Writers*

Let's analyze the life of Jonathan Edwards and see if we can identify the forces and principles that made him an exemplary Wavemaker whose actions and writings during his eighteenth-century lifetime continue making waves through the generations today.

Jonathan was born a British citizen in October 1703 in East Windsor, Connecticut, the fifth of eleven children and the only son of the Reverend Timothy Edwards and his wife, Esther. This was not the picturesque New England we know today; it was still rough and uncertain frontier land vulnerable to Indian attacks. Surrounded by stockade walls, villages looked like armed garrisons. England was at war with France, which increased the threat of Indian hostilities as the Indians joined forces with the French.

A product of Puritan heritage and an imposing and fiery preacher, Jonathan's maternal grandfather, Solomon Stoddard, believed that God was punishing New England because its citizens were violating His commandments. "God has had a great controversy with the country for many years," he preached. "We live in a corrupt age, and multitudes of men take a licentious liberty, in their drinking and apparel, and company, and recreations, and unsavory discourses."

Like all Puritans, Stoddard firmly believed that God had brought people to this promised land for His eternal purposes. A deep and constant student of the Bible, he understood well how God had dealt with his people in the Old Testament—with chastisements when they got out of line and blessings when they obeyed. He knew why they had suffered in captivity in Egypt for generations, and he was determined to do his part in preventing the judgments of God from bringing a similar fate to New Englanders.

Jonathan's father, Timothy, was a revivalist preacher. No one but Solomon Stoddard, Timothy's father-in-law, oversaw more local awakenings. A meticulous man and a strict disciplinarian, he took great care in the education of his children. Jonathan's mother, Esther, seems to have been a "woman of unusual mental gifts and independence of character."[5]

Jonathan recorded his first spiritual awakening at the age of nine. He prayed secretly five times a day and organized prayer meetings with other boys in his village. "My mind was much engaged in it," he later recalled, "and had much self-righteous pleasure; and it was my delight to abound in religious duties." With his schoolmates, he "built a booth in a swamp, in a very secret and retired place, for a place of prayer." But eventually that fervor passed, and he "entirely lost all those affections and delights" and "returned like a dog to his vomit, and went on in the ways of sin."[6] We can only imagine, tongue in check, how egregious his sins as a nine-year-old in Puritan New England could have been. Still, his journal entry exhibits his acute sensitivity to spiritual matters.

In the fall of 1716, at the age of thirteen, Jonathan left home to begin college in New Haven, Connecticut, in what is now Yale College, where he would eventually graduate as valedictorian of his class. A precocious and fastidious scholar, Jonathan thrived. But during his senior year, he fell deathly ill of pleurisy. His spiritual convictions were still forming, and he did not feel prepared to die. He later described his feelings, saying, "[God] shook me over the pit of hell."[7]

But after he recovered, his youthful tendencies prevailed, and, as had happened in his childhood, he "fell again into [his] old ways of sin." Like any typical sixteen-year-old boy, he resented the tedium of his parents' teaching and discipline. Living a life of holiness and rectitude seemed "a melancholy, morose, sour and unpleasant thing" to him. Church services bored him. He felt rebellious and proud, and he struggled with sexual lusts.[8]

He remained at New Haven to pursue an MA degree. While he soared intellectually, he struggled spiritually and continued wrestling with God. As he put it:

> God would not suffer me to go on with any quietness; but I had great and violent struggles: till after many conflicts with wicked inclinations, and repeated resolutions, and bonds that I laid myself under by a kind of vows to God, I was brought wholly to break off all former wicked ways, and all ways of known outward sin; and to apply myself to seek my salvation, and practice the duties of religions: but without that kind of affection and delight, that I had formerly experienced.[9]

Like Benjamin Franklin, Edwards created a series of resolutions to aid him in his efforts at self-discipline. By the time he turned twenty, he had written seventy personal resolutions. He read these resolutions once a week for thirty-five years—more than 1,800 times before his death.

As biographer A. C. McGiffert put it, "Deliberately he set about to temper his character into steel."

Consider a few of his resolutions below, which offer profound insights into his moral character and self-discipline as the foundations of his success[10]:

- *Resolved*, to do whatever I think to be my *duty*, and most for the good and advantage of mankind in general.
- *Resolved*, Never to lose one moment of time, but to improve it in the most profitable way I possibly can.
- *Resolved*, Never to do anything, which I should be afraid to do if it were the last hour of my life.
- *Resolved*, To inquire every night, as I am going to bed, wherein I have been negligent,—what sin I have committed,—and wherein I have denied myself;—also, at the end of every week, month, and year.
- *Resolved*, to ask myself, at the end of every day, week, month, and year, wherein I could possibly, in any respect, have done better.
- I frequently hear persons in old age say how they would live, if they were to live their lives over again: *Resolved*, That I will live just so as I can think I shall wish I had done, supposing I live to old age.
- *Resolved*, When I fear misfortunes and adversity, to examine whether I have done my duty, and resolve to do it and let the event be just as Providence orders it. I will, as far as I can, be concerned about nothing but my duty and my sin.

- *Resolved*, After afflictions, to inquire, what I am the better for them; what good I have got by them; and, what I might have got by them.

Also like Benjamin Franklin, Edwards held himself accountable to his resolutions and kept score daily in his diary. (To learn more about how Franklin and Edwards used resolutions to improve their lives and how you can do the same, see the book *RESOLVED: 13 Resolutions for LIFE* by Orrin Woodward.[11])

WAVEMAKER WISDOM

Self-discipline is the foundation of character, and character is the cornerstone of success. Creating personal resolutions, reading them daily, striving to abide by them, and holding yourself accountable to them is a powerful method for strengthening your self-discipline and molding your character.

Do you have personal resolutions written down? Do you read them frequently? Do you hold yourself accountable to them?

In his early years at college, his resolutions were more external reminders of duty than internalized, inspirational truths. In fact, he wrote in his later years that his rigorous adherence to his resolutions involved "too great a dependence on my own strength; which afterwards proved a great damage to me." He continued to struggle with the doctrines of salvation in what he termed a "miserable seeking." But as he aged and persevered through the struggle, he said, "I was brought to seek salvation, in a manner that I never was before."[12]

His spiritual breakthrough came at the age of seventeen as he was reading over and over again 1 Timothy 1:17 (NASB): "Now unto the King eternal, immortal, invisible, the only wise God, be honor and glory forever and ever. Amen." He later recalled that as he read these words, "There came into my soul, and was as it were diffused through it, a sense of the glory of the divine being; a new sense, quite different from anything I ever experienced before." He described his experience of repeating the verse as follows: "and as it were singing over these words of Scripture to myself...and prayed in a manner quite different from what I used to do; with a new sort of affection." His scripture study also took on greater depth, meaning, and intensity, his contemplations taking him into "a kind of vision...of being alone in the mountains, or some solitary wilderness, far from all mankind, sweetly conversing with Christ, and wrapped and swallowed up in God." He said, "[Spiritual raptures] would often of a sudden as it were, kindle up a sweet burning in my heart; an ardor of my soul, that I know not how to express."[13]

Soon after this transformation in college, he returned home for spring vacation and discussed his experiences with his father. After their conversation, he went for a walk in the woods alone. "As I was walking there," he related, "and looked upon the sky and clouds; there came into my mind, a sweet sense of the glorious majesty and grace of God, that I know not how to express." Edwards said from then on:

My sense of divine things gradually increased, and became more and more lively, and had more of that inward sweetness. The appearance of everything was altered: there seemed to be, as it were, a calm, sweet cast, or appearance of divine glory, in almost everything. God's excellency, his wisdom, his purity and love, seemed to appear in everything; in the sun, moon and stars; in the clouds; and blue sky; in the grass, flowers, and trees; in the water, and all nature."[14]

His spiritual renewal was thorough and complete, and he was ready to turn his life over to God.

WAVEMAKER WISDOM

The most important thing you can do as a leader is to develop an intimate relationship with God and submit your will to His. The more in tune to His will and willing to follow it that you are, the greater long-term impact you will have.

Have you been spiritually renewed? Have you dedicated your life to God? Do you actively seek to subvert your will to God's? Do you seek His guidance in your life daily through heartfelt prayer? Do you study His words daily?

Shortly after graduating Yale, Jonathan met a young woman, Sarah Pierpont, who would eventually become his wife and play an incalculable role in his success and that of his posterity. He provided insights into her character and temperament when he wrote of her at the time:

There is a young lady in New Haven who is beloved of that almighty Being, who made and rules the world...and this great Being...comes to her and fills her mind with exceeding sweet delight, and... she hardly cares for anything, except to meditate on him—that she expects after a while to be received up where he is, to be raised out of the world and caught up into heaven; being assured that he loves her too well to let her remain at a distance from him always....Therefore, if you present all the world before her, with the richest of its treasures, she disregards it and cares not for it, and is unmindful of any pain or affliction. She has a strange sweetness in her mind, and sweetness of temper, uncommon purity in her affections; is most just and praiseworthy in all her actions; and you could not persuade her to do anything thought wrong or sinful, if you would give her all the world, lest she should offend this great Being. She is of a wonderful sweetness, calmness and universal benevolence of mind....She will sometimes go about, singing sweetly, from place to place; and seems to be always full of joy and pleasure; and no one knows for what.[15]

In contrast to Sarah's perpetual joy, Jonathan struggled with bouts of depression throughout his life. His post-graduation decisions weighed so heavily on his mind that he had to check himself. He wrote in his diary during this time, "'Tis a most evil and pernicious practice in meditations on afflictions, to sit ruminating on the aggravations of the affliction, and reckoning up the evil, dark circumstances thereof, and dwelling long on the dark side; it doubles and trebles the affliction." The cure, he realized, was to think positively. As he put it, "If we dwelt on the light side of things in our thoughts, and extenuated them all that possibly we could, when speaking of them, we should think little of them ourselves; and the affliction would really, in a great measure, vanish away."[16]

WAVEMAKER WISDOM

Cultivating a positive attitude is critical to your long-term success. It helps you maintain hope and keeps your spirits up. It allows you to focus on solutions rather than problems.

How can you cultivate a more positive attitude, no matter how large and insurmountable your trials and challenges may seem?

After much introspection, Jonathan accepted a pastorate in the small hamlet of Bolton, Connecticut, which was near his hometown of East Windsor, on November 11, 1723. He quickly discovered that the townspeople bickered incessantly, and much of his focus was on keeping the peace. "We are but a little handful," he pleaded. "Christ has but a little flock; and shall his sheep devour one another?" From personal experience with resentments, he counseled, "By stepping a little back when we are resisted, the blow of the enemy loses its force, as a woolsack stops and deadens a bullet sooner than an oak tree because it gives way. So a man of a meek and mild temper kills strife sooner than he that resists."[17]

In May of the following year, Edwards received the news that Yale had offered him a position as a tutor. Once again, the decision weighed him down, particularly because he knew that Yale students were notorious for drinking and rowdiness, which affected his spiritual sensitivities. Soon after his arrival in New Haven, he wrote in his diary, "This week has been a remarkable week with me in respect to despondencies, fears, perplexities, multitudes of cares and distraction of mind....I have now abundant reason to be convinced of the troublesomeness and vexation of the world, and that it never will be another kind of world."[18]

Although Jonathan enjoyed tutoring his students, during commencement week of 1724, he experienced a devastating test of faith, the cause of which is unclear from his personal writings and from which it took him three years to recover. He wrote in his diary:

> Saturday night, Sept 12. Crosses of the nature of that, which I met with this week, thrust me below all comforts in religion. They appear no more than vanity and stubble, especially when I meet with them so unprepared for them. I shall not be fit to encounter them, except I have a far stronger, and more permanent faith, hope and love.

Jonathan found it difficult to concentrate during prayers and felt spiritually dead.[19]

He trudged on with firm resolution and guarded hope. On May 28, 1725, he wrote in resignation:

> It seems to me, that whether I am now converted or not, I am so settled in the state I am in, that I shall go on in it all my life. But however settled I may be, yet I will continue to pray to God, not to suffer me to be deceived about it, nor to sleep in an unsafe condition; and ever and anon, will call all into question and try myself, using for helps, some of our old divines, that God may have opportunities to answer my prayers, and the spirit of God to show me my error, if I am in one.[20]

One bright light shone through his life at this time, and that was his blossoming relationship with Sarah Pierpont.

Although Sarah was only fifteen, they got engaged that summer, with a wedding date set for two years later. Obviously, two years of sexual tension would try the resolve of the most virtuous. Edwards alluded to struggling with his thoughts and revealed his solution for dealing with unworthy ones:

> When one suppresses thoughts that tend to divert the run of the mind's operations from religion, whether they are melancholy, or anxious, or passionate, or any others; there is this good effect of it, that it keeps the mind in its freedom. Those thoughts are stopped in the beginning, that would have set the mind a-going in that stream.[21]

In the spring of 1726, a great opportunity arose for Jonathan. He was asked to serve as an assistant to his grandfather, Solomon Stoddard, in the Northampton, Massachusetts, congregation. In a town meeting, he was voted into the position on November 21, 1726, and was officially ordained to the position on February 15, 1727. In July 1727, he and Sarah were finally married, and they moved to Northampton. By fall of that year, he felt recovered from his spiritual drought, writing, "'Tis just about three years, that I have been for the most part in a low, sunk estate and condition, miserably senseless to what I used to be, about spiritual things." On August 25, 1728, Sarah bore their first child, a daughter whom they also named Sarah.[22]

WAVEMAKER WISDOM

Low points are a natural and inevitable part of life. You *will* experience dark times, when you cannot see the light, your path is unclear, and the way seems to be "hedged up." During those times, press on with firm resolve. The light *will* come. The path *will* be revealed!
How can you motivate yourself when life is difficult?

When Solomon Stoddard died in February of 1729, Jonathan found himself responsible for the spiritual and moral oversight of about 1,300 congregants. The shoes he had to fill were huge; for decades, Solomon Stoddard had been referred to as the "pope of the Connecticut valley." Jonathan was newly-married, had just become a father, had assumed the full duties of pastor and was preaching three times a week, and was also working on a number of writing projects. Under the anxiety of the transition and the strain of too much work, his health collapsed, which would prove to be a recurring theme throughout his life.

After a much-needed recovery period, he threw himself back into the work of saving souls. After more than four years of patiently and diligently cultivating the spiritual garden of his congregation, the blossoms of the First Great Awakening appeared. It was reported that several families were swept up by "a remarkable religious concern," and "a number of persons seemed to be savingly wrought upon." The real turning point came in April 1734 when a young man suddenly died, which had a profound effect on the young people of Jonathan's congregation.[23]

Biographer George Marsden writes that "Edwards' whole life had prepared him to seize this moment. Having been twice on the verge of death, he had spent much of his own youth reflecting on the folly of loving earthly pleasure when on the brink of eternity."[24]

When another died, this time a young married woman, the speed and intensity of the awakening increased. By fall, it had spread and transformed the youth culture of Northampton. Edwards directed the townspeople to begin holding prayer meetings in small groups throughout the week, thus reviving one of the fundamental components of the Puritan movement.

WAVEMAKER WISDOM

You never know what life will bring, what opportunities will be presented to you, what challenges to expect. Live your life so as to be prepared to conquer challenges and seize opportunities as they arise. Cultivate your character consistently. Learn lessons from your experiences, always with an eye toward future application. Build relationships. Gather assets.

Remember the advice from Winston Churchill, "To each there comes in their lifetime a special moment when they are figuratively tapped on the shoulder and offered the chance to do a very special thing, unique to them and fitted to their talents. What a tragedy if that moment finds them unprepared or unqualified for that which could have been their finest hour."

How are you preparing for your future? What more should you be doing? What knowledge should you be gaining? What skills should you be learning? What character traits should you be developing? What relationships should you be building?

In December, the flames of the awakening were fanned into a great inferno when a young woman, notorious as "one of the greatest company-keepers in the whole town," came to Edwards to report her spiritual conversion, convincing him that "what she gave an account of was glorious work of God's infinite power and sovereign grace."[25]

By March of 1735, the spiritual fervor of the awakening reached its highest point, and "a great and earnest concern about the great things of religion and the eternal world became universal in all parts of the town, and among persons of all degrees and all ages," as Edwards reported.[26] He proclaimed to the world in *A Faithful Narrative*, that "there has been a great and marvelous work of conversion and sanctification among the people here."

Edwards worked diligently to harness the energy of the awakening and ensure that those affected by it maintained their spiritual dedication. His leadership role in the revival spread as far as England and Scotland. The next few years saw something of a cooling of the religious fervor, until Edwards set out on a revival tour with fellow preacher George Whitefield.

In 1741, while on tour with Whitefield, Edwards preached his most famous sermon, "Sinners in the Hands of an Angry God," in Enfield, Connecticut. Although the content of the speech was "fire and brimstone," Edwards was not a charismatic, emotional speaker. One observer wrote:

> [His delivery style was] easy, natural and very solemn. He had not a strong, loud voice; but appeared with such gravity and solemnity, and spake with such distinctness, clearness and precision; his words were so full of ideas, set in such a plain and striking light, that few speakers have been able to demand the attention of an audience as he.

The audience was so moved that, as one observer reported, "there was a great moaning and crying out throughout the whole house. 'What shall I do to be saved? Oh, I am going to Hell! Oh, what shall I do for Christ?'" Edwards had to stop and ask for silence in order to be heard, but the cries only increased. As he waited, the wails increased, and he never finished the sermon. It was reported that "Several souls were hopefully wrought upon that night, and oh the cheerfulness and pleasantness of their countenances."[27]

In March 1742, Northampton was at the peak of another revival. After witnessing that some of the emotions expressed during the earlier awakening were superficial, Edwards wanted to ensure long-term commitments from his converts.

He wrote a church covenant and presented it to leading members of his congregation, winning their approval. He declared Tuesday, March 16, 1742, as a day of fasting, prayer, and covenant-making. The whole congregation assembled in the meetinghouse, and in a solemn ceremony, every church member over the age of fourteen rose and agreed to the covenant, in which they covenanted "to avoid all unchristian inveighings, reproachings, bitter reflectings, judging and ridiculing others," among many other things. The youth covenanted "that we will strictly avoid all freedoms and familiarities in company, so tending either to stir up or gratify a lust of lasciviousness." Everyone also promised to "devote our whole lives to be laboriously spent in the business of religion" and to "run with perseverance the race that is set before us."[28]

WAVEMAKER WISDOM

As a leader, you must capture the emotions of the people you serve and harness them into long-term commitments. Everyone gets excited at big events, but the rubber hits the road when they go home and they're all alone.

How can get your followers to make and keep commitments?

Under Edwards's leadership, for the next few years, the people of Northampton enjoyed an abundance of spiritual blessings. But much of what Edwards had struggled to build for the past fifteen years came crashing down in one small-town controversy. In March 1744, Edwards learned that a number of young men in his congregation had been passing around medical books and making lewd jokes about the female anatomy found therein. The young men, it was reported, had also been sexually harassing young women using material about menstruation found in the books.

Edwards quickly formed a committee of brethren to help him manage the affair and, hopefully, defuse the situation and set the young men straight. But in doing so, Edwards made a fateful mistake. Over the pulpit, he announced when the committee would meet at his house and read off a list of people ordered to report at the meeting. The list included some of the accused and some who were only witnesses, but Edwards failed to differentiate between them, thus implying fault in all of them. By the time the committee met, "the town was suddenly all on a blaze."[29]

The incident created a lot of resentment toward Edwards because, as George Marsden wrote:

> Edwards was attributing momentous importance to behavior that looked trivial, even if childish and distasteful, to many other inhabitants of the town. The more he made of it, the more he lost support. Hopkins remarks that as a result of this incident Edwards "greatly lost his influence," especially

among young people, and that "this seemed in a great measure to put an end to Mr. Edwards' usefulness at Northampton." Edwards himself later referred to it as that "which gave so great offense, and by which I became so obnoxious."[30]

WAVEMAKER WISDOM

When you have a concern about the behavior or performance of any people you serve, discuss it with them privately. Never embarrass people in public; this does nothing but create resentment and hostility. Don't let lackluster performance or inappropriate behavior slide, but handle admonishments with love and respect.

Are there any behavioral issues among your team that should be addressed? How can you handle them lovingly and judiciously?

Edwards's relationship with his congregation never recovered after this incident. Not much later, a dispute over his salary deepened resentments among congregants. When his uncle, Colonel John Stoddard, died unexpectedly on June 26, 1748, he lost one of his most important allies, and his relationship with the town was further eroded, thus prefacing one of the most famous events of his career.

When Edwards began repudiating his grandfather Stoddard's views on communion, wanting to require a much stricter standard than had been applied under Solomon's tenure, the spark of resentment burst into the flame of outrage. Edwards wrote a treatise to explain his views, which were, if nothing else, motivated by a deeply sincere commitment to fully living the gospel of Christ. But few townspeople would read it; nor would they allow Edwards to hold a public debate or preach on the subject. The leader, fully committed to Christ and wishing to raise his congregants to a higher level of commitment, found himself at odds with his followers, who had become accustomed to more liberal standards.

By December of 1749, the majority of people in the town and church were pushing hard for Edwards's removal as pastor. Eventually, after much controversy, a vote was called, and only 23 of the 230 male members of the congregation voted in favor of keeping Edwards as pastor. However, the council exonerated him from accusations of a lack of sincerity and integrity in the matter, concluding that he was "uprightly following the dictates of his own conscience." They commended him for his "[C]hristian spirit and temper" and then declared him to be "eminently qualified for the work of the Gospel ministry"—that is, in any church that shared his views.[31]

It was noted that Edwards's demeanor was remarkably calm throughout the inflammatory proceedings. As one supporter wrote:

I never saw the least symptoms of displeasure in his countenance the whole week, but he appeared like a man of God, whose happiness was out of the reach of his enemies, and whose treasure was not only a future but a present good, overbalancing all imaginable ills of life, even to the astonishment of many, who could not be at rest without his dismission.[32]

Though Edwards's timing was poor, his courage and integrity are commendable. He was willing to stand on principle against popular opinion, even when it cost him personally.

WAVEMAKER WISDOM

There's a huge difference between leadership and demagoguery. Leadership requires making tough choices, which often go against the grain of popular opinion. Leadership is about doing what's right, not giving people what they want.

How are you standing firm against popular opinion? Are you being effective in promoting your views?

After being ousted by his congregation, Jonathan accepted a pastorate in Stockbridge, Massachusetts, with the joint job of teaching and evangelizing local Mahican (or Mohican) Indians, in June of 1751. He spent the next few years ministering to the Indians and writing, until an Indian uprising effectively brought his mission to its knees.

In the spring of 1757, he was asked to replace his son-in-law, Aaron Burr (the father of the infamous Aaron Burr who killed Alexander Hamilton in a duel), as president of Princeton University. He was installed as president on February 16, 1758. Almost immediately after becoming president, he died from the effects of a smallpox inoculation on March 22, 1758, at the age of fifty-four. His beloved Sarah followed him in death shortly thereafter, on October 2, 1758, at the age of forty-eight.

Jonathan's final words on his deathbed, spoken to his daughter Lucy, reveal a critical component of the Edwards legacy we have not touched on thus far:

> Dear Lucy, it seems to me to be the will of God that I must shortly leave you; therefore give my kindest love to my dear wife, and tell her, that the uncommon union, which has long subsisted between us, has been of such a nature, as I trust is spiritual, and therefore will continue forever: and I hope she will be supported under so great a trial, and submit cheerfully to the will of God. And as to my children, you are now like to be left fatherless, which I hope will be an inducement to you all to seek a Father, who will never fail you.

That "uncommon union" with Sarah and her contributions to their family were every bit as important to their family legacy as anything Jonathan ever did. Like every famous man, Jonathan's contributions were catalyzed and supported by and dependent upon those of his dear wife. As Albert Winship wrote:

> Mrs. Edwards lived in her children. To her husband came honor and glory in his lifetime, but to her came denial, toil and care. At eighteen, this young, beautiful, brilliant wife became a mother, and until she was forty, there was never a period of two years in which a child was not born to them, and no one of the eleven children died until after the last child was born. It was a home of little children. Her husband had no care for the household and she wished him to have none. It was her insistence that he should have thirteen hours of every twenty-four for his study. Whatever may have been the contribution of Mr. Edwards to the inheritance of the family, they owed the charming environment of the home to their mother.[33]

George Whitefield, a contemporary preacher of Jonathan Edwards, wrote in his diary that he "sometimes wondered if it was not the Lord's will that he should marry, that he might thereby be more useful, and that if it was the Lord's will that he should marry, he...did hope that the Lord would send him as a wife such a woman as Mrs. Edwards, whom he considered the most beautiful and noble wife for a Christian minister that he had ever known."[34]

Samuel Hopkins, who frequently stayed in the Edwards home and had much occasion to observe Sarah with her children, wrote a glowing tribute to Sarah in his biography of Edwards. He described her as "a more than ordinary beautiful person; of a pleasant, agreeable countenance" and as having "the law of kindness on her tongue." She displayed much charity for the poor and extraordinary kindness to guests and strangers. She "paid proper deference to Mr. Edwards" while frequently laboring under "bodily disorders and pains." Hopkins also noted:

> She had an excellent way of governing her children; she knew how to make them regard and obey her cheerfully. She seldom punished them, and in speaking to them used gentle and pleasant words. When she had occasion to reprove or rebuke, she would do it in a few words, without warmth and noise, and with all calmness and gentleness of mind. In her directions and reproofs of matters of importance, she would address herself to the reason of her children, that they might not only know her inclination and will, but at the same time be convinced of the reasonableness of it. She had need to speak but once and she was obeyed; murmuring and answering again were not known among them....
>
> Quarreling and contention were in her family wholly unknown. She carefully observed the first appearance of resentment and ill will in her young children towards any person whatever, and did not connive at it, but was careful to show her displeasure, and suppress it to the utmost; yet not by angry, wrathful words.

Her system of discipline began at a very early age, and it was her rule to resist the first, as well as every subsequent exhibition of temper or disobedience in the child, however young, until its will was brought into submission to the will of the parents.[35]

Though Sarah did not share the pulpit with Edwards, she deserves as much, if not more, of the credit for his legacy. The renowned success of their posterity was not due to the influence of a pious father alone but also to the nurturing of a loving mother.

WAVEMAKER WISDOM

Religious leader David O. McKay wrote, "No other success can compensate for failure in the home." Next to your duties to God, your first and foremost duty is to nurture, strengthen, protect, serve, and build your family, beginning with cultivating your relationship with your spouse. Indeed, your relationship with your spouse will have the greatest impact on your performance in your career and leadership efforts.

Are you actively and consistently strengthening and deepening your relationship with your spouse? Are you giving him or her the respect, love, and time that he or she needs? Are you fulfilling your duties to your children? Does your commitment to your family show in the time and energy you spend with them?

The impact of Jonathan and Sarah Edwards's legacy is incalculable. Their dedication to God, family, and principle produced waves that will be felt through eternity. They demonstrate that of all the legacies we can leave, a righteous posterity is by far the greatest.

CHAPTER THREE

A SOCIAL REVOLUTION ON BEHALF OF THE "FORGOTTEN CITIZEN"

Education is not the filling of a pail, but the lighting of a fire.

—WILLIAM BUTLER YEATS

In the late 1870s, a bored and frustrated little girl named Maria sat at her desk in an elementary school in a small Italian town, doing her best to memorize the biographies of famous women. Her teacher was adamant about the exercise in order to, as Maria put it, "incite us to imitate them."

"You too should try to become famous," her teacher exhorted. "Would you not like to become famous?"

"Oh, no," Maria retorted, "I shall never be that. I care too much for the children of the future to add yet another biography to the list."

Little did the witty child know at the time what an amazing biography she would eventually add to the pages of history.

In 1870, after a century of being considered the backwater of Western Europe, Italy was transforming under the guidance of social reformers. A new, liberal coalition government was pushing the extension of voting rights, greater civil liberties, a more equalized tax system, and the development of public education.

But despite these efforts, Italy's society remained deeply stratified. Strangling regulations and rigid bureaucracy held the economy hostage. The government frequently violated freedom of the press. Strikes were illegal. Administrative corruption was rampant. Three quarters of the population over ten could neither read nor write. Most citizens were destitute. Child labor was prevalent. Public schools were primarily attended by boys, and educated females were rare in the male-dominated culture. Typical schools were crowded and dirty, presided over by schoolmasters or mistresses earning as little as $120 per year. Few books or teaching materials were provided. The standard pedagogy was performing drills.

Married women could not legally write checks on their own account; their money was the property of their husbands. They could not give evidence in a court of law without their husband's presence. It was not considered proper for women of any age, married or single, to go out on the streets alone.

Though revolution was brewing, it would take decades for the dreams of reformers to be realized. It was into this environment that Maria Montessori was born in a little town called Chiaravalle in 1870. Her father, Alessandro, was a successful government official involved in the financial management of the state-run tobacco industry, a respectable member of bourgeois society. Her mother hailed from a landed family and was unusually well educated. In 1875, the family moved to Rome, where they would remain.

Though little Maria was not academically precocious, she was, by all accounts, self-confident, strong-willed, and a little bossy. In short, she was a natural-born leader with a maverick personality, which would serve her well later in life. In spite of her bossiness, she was also a peacemaker. On one occasion, her parents were involved in a heated argument. Maria dragged a chair to a position between them, climbed up on it, and then joined their hands together.

As she aged, she discovered that she learned easily and performed well on exams. She began studying intensely, even taking books with her to the theater, where she would study in the dim light during performances. She had a loving relationship with her father, but it was her mother, Renilde, who provided the most support.

Thanks to Renilde's encouragement, Maria enthusiastically read books and asked questions. By the age of fourteen, after discovering an aptitude for mathematics, she decided that she wanted to become an engineer, which was unheard of for a woman at that time. So she began attending a technical school for boys.

Similar to most schools in Italy at the time, the school was a rigid, conformist "conveyor-belt." Everyone was taught the same material at the same time and moved at the same pace. They were expected to simply memorize lectures, rather than question and debate what was taught. Discipline was strictly enforced, with harsh penalties imposed for getting out of line. The environment was not in the slightest conducive to independent thinking, nor did it foster a love of learning. Furthermore, during recess, the girl students were not allowed to mix with the boys, so they spent the period shut off in a room by themselves.

But Maria had been born with an unusual capacity to resist conformity and form her own judgments. As biographer Rita Kramer wrote, "Only a certain eccentricity of mind and a forceful character could survive such a system with the ability to see things freshly and reassemble the elements of experience in novel ways. It is usually called genius, and it is what Montessori had."[1]

She graduated from the technical school in the spring of 1886 with excellent grades in all her subjects. Her plans to become an engineer were interrupted by what her friend later called a "mystical experience," through which she felt prompted to study medicine instead. "She herself cannot explain how it came about," her friend reported.

It happened all in a moment. She was walking in a street when she passed a woman with a baby holding a long, narrow, red strip of paper. I have heard Dr. Montessori describe this little street scene and the decision that then came to her. At such times there was in her eyes a long deep look, as if she were searching out things which were far beyond words. Then she would say, "Why?" and with a little expressive movement of her hand indicate that there are strange things happening within us guiding us toward an end we do not know.[2]

This would not be the last time Maria would make a critical life decision so suddenly and intuitively. It was a hallmark of her life.

WAVEMAKER WISDOM

The left hemisphere of the human brain is logical, rational, sequential, and deductive. It views the world legalistically, in black-and-white terms, seeing everything as either correct or incorrect, right or wrong, true or false. In most people, the left hemisphere is domineering and won't allow them to accept as reality anything it can't see, test, measure, and validate.

But often in life, hunches, premonitions, and gut feelings allude to deeper truths than the left brain can see. This is the right brain, the seat of intuition, at work. Where the left brain wants to pick things apart and analyze one detail at a time at a microscopic level, the right brain perceives the whole picture simultaneously.

The right brain recognizes patterns and sees connections that the left brain cannot see.

This is why right-brain geniuses are considered fools by left-brain people. Study the geniuses in history, and you'll find that they were in tune with and listened to their right brains. Thus, they saw things that most people couldn't see. They followed their gut feelings down deep rabbit holes to see where they would lead, even when people called them crazy for doing so.

Are you in tune with your intuition? Do you trust and follow your flashes of insight from your right-brain genius when you receive them, or do you allow your left-brain lawyer to stifle them? What intuitions have you followed in the past, and what did they lead to? What intuitions have you ignored, and what were the consequences?

Maria's father and other relatives and friends of the family were shocked and disapproving of her decision to study medicine. Her goal was considered preposterous and impossible. Her father did not forbid her outright, however, and so she made an appointment to see Guido Baccelli, a professor of medicine at the University of Rome. Mr. Baccelli firmly refused to encourage her to apply for admission to medical school. But as she was leaving, Maria declared, "I *know* I shall become a doctor."[3]

She enrolled at the University of Rome in the fall of 1890 at the age of twenty for physics, mathematics, and natural sciences classes. While other young women her age were reading romances, she was engrossed in thick volumes of zoology, botany, physics, and chemistry. She passed her exams in 1892 with a final grade of eight out of a possible ten points, making her eligible to move on to medical school.

Her ambition was both unprecedented and unthinkable. But supported by her mother, Maria persisted until she was accepted. She soon discovered that getting accepted would be the least of her challenges. The jealous male students, their pride threatened, pestered her incessantly and did everything they could to make her life miserable.

Over time, however, their persecution changed to admiration as she responded with good humor and pursued her goal with single-minded determination. When passing her in the halls, many of the students would give her a contemptuous "*Pooh!*" She would cheerfully reply, "Blow away, my friends; the harder you blow, the higher up I shall go."[4]

One professor shared a story that revealed Maria's dedication. One day when he was due to lecture, a tremendous snowstorm swept over Rome. The blizzard was so severe that he didn't expect anyone to show up. But as he arrived in class, he found one lone girl sitting in the lecture room: Maria Montessori. Maria suggested that perhaps he should postpone his lecture. But the professor would not let her zeal go unrewarded and delivered his lecture to an audience of one.

WAVEMAKER WISDOM

So much of success in life is simply showing up. Talk is cheap. Natural talent is overrated. As painter Chuck Close said, "Inspiration is for amateurs—the rest of us just show up and get to work." Success follows those who consistently show up: the front-row sitters, the trench diggers, the people who volunteer to do the tough, unglamorous work that others don't want to do. As the poet Longfellow put it:

Heights by great men reached and kept
Were not obtained by sudden flight but,
While their companions slept,
They were toiling upward in the night.[5]

Are you showing up in life? Are you volunteering to do the work that others don't want to do? Are you doing the things most people are unwilling to do so that you can enjoy things most people will never have?

Determined and spunky as she was, even Maria was subject to doubt and discouragement. At one point in her schooling, she hit a wall. All her struggles—her father's opposition, the hostility of her fellow students, the burden of combating social norms—seemed too much to bear. She left the dissecting room depressed one evening, resolved to quit and pursue a different career.

On her way home, she walked through a nearly deserted park, where she was approached by a dirty beggar woman dressed in rags. The woman was accompanied by a child of about two years old. While the woman asked Maria for money, the child sat on the ground playing with a small piece of colored paper. Something in the child's blissful expression held Maria mesmerized. He was perfectly content, totally absorbed in play with a worthless scrap of paper.

Her dear friend E. M. Standing, her first biographer, related what Maria told him about the experience: "Moved by emotions she could not herself explain, she turned round, and went straight back to the dissecting room. From that moment her revulsion to the work in those uncongenial surroundings left her, never to return. From that moment, too, she never doubted that she had a vocation."[6]

Another friend and biographer, Anna Maccheroni, recalled Maria speaking of the experience:

> She does feel that there are results from what we are and what we do which are not chosen by us as we choose so many things on the surface of our lives.... In one of her lectures she spoke of man's superior mission of which he is not aware. She instanced the corals. They, tiny as they are, can have no outlook beyond their own life. Yet, as a result of their living, new islands and even new continents are born. "We human beings," she said, "we must have a mission, too, of which we are not aware." When she spoke

of the sudden change in her life plans I could feel an inner certitude which made her persevere against her father's strong opposition and all the other difficulties that beset her path.[7]

Maria said of the experience, "I cannot explain it. It just happened like that. You will probably think it a very silly story: and if you told it to others they would probably just laugh at it."[8]

"In this we see an example," wrote Standing, "of that mysterious affinity which exists, deep down in the soul of the genius, towards that work which he is destined to perform, and everything connected with it."[9] That "mysterious affinity" is intuition; Maria was bursting with it, and she trusted it to guide her throughout her life.

Not for many years would Maria find her ultimate life's mission in education. But as she preached in her later years, "the preparations of life are indirect." Standing explained:

> I once heard her expound on a theory that the art of life consists in learning how "to be obedient to events." Superficially this might give the impression of a fatalistic surrender to an external destiny; but it meant nothing of the kind. Rightly understood, and illustrated as she gave it by reference to her own career, it signified rather a life full of generous acceptances of duties, and of hard achievements leading to unexpected developments along the line of her genius. Thus it came about that her life was like a path leading through narrow defiles to sudden

horizons; a series of experiences linking themselves together to prepare the next step.[10]

Her devotion to medicine would later open doors for her, through which she would walk to find her true purpose.

WAVEMAKER WISDOM

The twentieth-century genius Buckminster Fuller coined the term "precession," which he defined as "the effect of bodies in motion on other bodies in motion." Put more simply, it is the indirect result(s) of someone's direct actions. For example, the direct goal of honeybees is to gather nectar to make honey. The precessional, indirect effect is cross-pollination.

Very often in life, we don't know what the results of our actions will be. But as we stay in motion and follow intuition, one thing leads to another, and experiences build on each other, culminating in a powerful mission.

If you don't have absolute clarity on your life's purpose, just choose a worthy goal and work with all your heart and soul to achieve it. What matters isn't the accomplishment of that goal but rather what that pursuit leads you to. The long-term, unseen, precessional effects of pursuing goals are far more powerful than the actual goals themselves.

> *Are you pursuing worthy goals right now? Are they clearly defined? Are you keeping an open mind to see what that pursuit may lead to?*

Soon after this experience, Maria became so sick that her friends were seriously concerned about her recovery. "Do not be alarmed," she told them. "I shall not die; I have work to do."

She continued her studies, supported and encouraged by her mother at home. Her relationship with her father took a happy turn when, at the end of her final year of medical school, she was asked to give a lecture. Though she was fully expecting her fellow students to create a disturbance, she was pleased that they were quiet and attentive. More important, her father was in attendance. She received a standing ovation, and her father was so proud of her that his opposition to her goals immediately ceased. From then on, he was one of her greatest supporters.

In 1896, Maria graduated with honors and became the first woman in Italy to acquire the degree of Doctor of Medicine. When she was given her diploma, many of the words printed on the document had to be changed in pen and ink from the masculine to the feminine (for example, *dal Signore* to *dalla Signora*). The elaborate document had not been designed for females.

After graduation Maria was appointed assistant doctor at the psychiatric clinic at the University of Rome. As part of her duties, she visited asylums for the insane to select suitable subjects for the clinic. In one of these asylums, she saw mentally handicapped children who were kept like prisoners. They saw no one but each other; they did nothing but stare, sleep, and eat. Their caretaker did not conceal her disgust for them. When Maria asked her why she held them in such contempt, she answered, "Because as soon as their meals are finished they throw themselves on the floor to search for the crumbs."[11]

Maria looked around the room and saw that they had no toys or materials of any kind; the room was utterly bare. It dawned on her that the children were not starved for food, but rather for stimulation and experience. They were grabbing at the crumbs as children grab for toys as their only means of relieving the awful boredom. Their minds were not useless, but unused, she concluded.

She pondered on the plight of those children as she continued her work with private patients as well as at the hospitals and psychiatric clinic. She began to read everything she could find on mentally defective children, and that search led her to the works of the French physician Jean-Marc-Gaspard Itard and his disciple Edouard Seguin. Itard had gained notoriety for his studies with a deaf-mute twelve-year-old boy who had been found running wild in the woods. His work with that boy and other deaf-mutes and mentally handicapped children showed that the children could learn, communicate, and interact. After studying his work, Maria concluded that "mental deficiency presented chiefly a pedagogical, rather than mainly a medical, problem."[12] In short, she felt the children could be helped by special methods of education. She said:

That form of creation, which was necessary for these unfortunate beings, so as to enable them to reenter human society, to take their place in the civilized world and render them independent of the help of others—placing human dignity within their grasp—was a work which appealed so strongly to my heart that I remained in it for years.[13]

Between 1897 and 1898, she immersed herself in the study of every major work on educational theory from the previous two hundred years. From that study emerged her own theories of education, as well as a detailed plan for helping mentally handicapped children integrate more fully into society. When she began lecturing on her ideas, she caught the attention of the minister of education.

Before long, a state-sponsored institution was built, and Maria was asked to be the director. She accepted the position and began working directly with the children from 8:00 a.m. to 7:00 p.m. every day. At night she would make notes and then analyze and compare them. She was thrilled, but not surprised, to see tangible improvement in her children. She wrote:

We must know how to call to the *man* which lies dormant within the soul of the child. I felt this, intuitively, and believed that not the didactic material, but my voice which called to them, *awakened* the children, and encouraged them to use the didactic material, and through it, to educate themselves. I was guided in my work by the deep respect which I felt for their misfortune, and by the love which these unhappy children know how to awaken in those who are near them.[14]

As she served in that position for two years, she began realizing that the methods she was using could and should be applied with equal success on a broader scale, to children of all abilities and ages, not just the mentally handicapped. She reflected:

> Whilst everyone was admiring my [mentally handicapped children], I was searching for the reasons which could keep back the healthy and happy children of ordinary schools on so low a plane that they could be equaled in tests of intelligence by my unfortunate pupils....I became convinced that similar methods applied to normal children would develop or set free their personality in a marvelous and surprising way.[15]

In 1901, she resigned from the school, citing the need for further study and personal reflection. Although she was already a lecturer at the University of Rome, she enrolled again as a student to take philosophy and psychology courses. She explained this period in her life in a letter to a young teacher she mentored: "To collect one's forces, even when they seem to be scattered, and when one's aim is only dimly perceived—this is a great action and will sooner or later bring forth fruits....It was almost as if I was keeping myself for an unknown mission."[16]

WAVEMAKER WISDOM

Periodic retreats can help us gather our energy, reflect on our goals, and gain clarity on our purpose. As Chris Brady teaches in his book *A Month of Italy: Rediscovering the Art of Vacation*, "Sometimes you have to go slow in order to go fast."[17]

This is what Stephen R. Covey calls "sharpening the saw" in his book *The 7 Habits of Highly Effective People*. He explains:

> Sharpen the Saw means preserving and enhancing the greatest asset you have — you. It means having a balanced program for self-renewal in the four areas of your life: physical, social/emotional, mental, and spiritual....As you renew yourself in each of the four areas, you create growth and change in your life. Sharpen the Saw keeps you fresh so you can continue to practice the other six habits. You increase your capacity to produce and handle the challenges around you. Without this renewal, the body becomes weak, the mind mechanical, the emotions raw, the spirit insensitive, and the person selfish.[18]

Are you taking time to "sharpen the saw"?

The more Maria studied, the more interested she became in education. In 1904, she was asked to teach a course to teachers on the history of anthropology and its application to education. She told her young teachers, "The subject of our study is humanity; our purpose is to become teachers. Now, what really makes a teacher is love for the human child; for it is love that transforms the social duty of the educator into the higher consciousness of a *mission*."[19]

By 1906, Montessori was, at thirty-six years old, an established professional, a distinguished scientist and academic who was well known and highly regarded by a wide circle of civic and social leaders. She had paid the price for an education and felt ready to begin applying her theories and methods on a broad scale.

An opportunity arose when she was approached by a group of wealthy bankers, the directors of the Roman Real Estate Association, to aid them in an urban renewal scheme. After years of neglect, the San Lorenzo district of Rome had become a slum plagued by poverty and crime. The association had renovated a few of the buildings in the district to provide apartments for poor working families.

Among the families of the people who moved into the renovated apartments were about sixty children. Left to their own devices while their parents worked during the day, these children, who were old enough to get around but too young for school, ran wild through the building, defacing freshly painted walls and vandalizing the building. The builders were desperate to do something to protect their investment. They decided to gather the children in one place and keep them there throughout the day.

They asked Montessori to preside over what was essentially a daycare in a slum.

Maria accepted—to the dismay of her professional colleagues. This was unthinkable for a university professor. One of her chiefs in the medical school condescendingly chastised her for "lowering the prestige of the medical profession." Maria, however, was no stranger to bucking social norms.

Whenever you buck the status quo, be prepared for criticism. As Winston Churchill said, "You have enemies? Good. That means you've stood up for something, sometime in your life." Elbert Hubbard expressed the reverse, "To avoid criticism, do nothing, say nothing, and be nothing."

Are you taking a noteworthy stand for a great cause? Do you welcome criticism as evidence of effectiveness?

Maria described seeing the children for the first time:

Sixty tearful, frightened children, so shy that it was impossible to get them to speak; their faces were expressionless, with bewildered eyes as though they had never seen anything in their lives…poor abandoned children who had grown up in dark tumbledown cottages without anything to stimulate their minds—dejected, uncared for. It was not necessary to be a doctor to see that they suffered from malnutrition, lack of fresh air and sunlight. They were indeed closed flowers, but without the freshness of buds, souls concealed in a hermetic cell.[20]

On the opening day, the sixth of January, 1906, Maria said she "had a strange feeling which made me announce emphatically that here was the opening of an undertaking of which the whole world would one day speak."[21] It would not take long for the world to start speaking of Maria and her work with the children of the slum. Everything up to this point in her life had prepared her for this moment. She wrote:

> I set to work like a peasant woman who, having set aside a good store of seed corn, has found a fertile field in which she may freely sow it. But I was wrong. I had hardly turned over the clods of my field, when I found gold instead of wheat: the clods concealed a precious treasure. I was not the peasant I had thought myself. Rather I was like foolish Aladdin, who, without knowing it, had in his hand a key that would open hidden treasures.[22]

Maria was still occupied with teaching, research, and a medical practice, so she hired an assistant—specifically chosen without an educational background to ensure that she would not be prejudiced and bound by old methods of teaching. Maria brought in teaching materials she had developed with the mentally handicapped children and asked her assistant to make them available to the children.

"I placed no restrictions upon the teacher and imposed no special duties," she wrote. "I merely wanted to study the children's reactions. I asked her not to interfere with them in any way as otherwise I would not be able to observe them."[23] Some friends donated a few toys, and Maria also procured paper and colored pencils.

Within mere weeks, the children showed remarkable improvement, both academically and socially. "From timid and wild as they were before," Maria observed, "the children became sociable and communicative. They showed different relationships with each other. Their personalities grew and they showed extraordinary understanding, activity, vivacity, and confidence. They were happy and joyous."

She shared one experience of teaching the children how to blow their noses:

> After I had shown them different ways to use a handkerchief, I ended by indicating how it could be done as unobtrusively as possible. I took out my handkerchief in such a way that they could hardly see it and blew my nose as softly as I could. The children watched me in rapt attention, but failed to laugh. I wondered why, but I had hardly finished my demonstration when they broke out into applause that resembled a long repressed ovation in a theater.[24]

Maria realized that, though trivial to her, the lesson was sensitive to the children, who were constantly being scolded for having runny noses but had never been taught how to use a handkerchief. "They felt compensated for past humiliations," She explained, "and their applause indicated that I had not only treated them with justice but had enabled them to get a new standing in society." By treating the children with respect, she had earned their trust and unlocked their latent abilities.[25]

Ever going against the grain, Maria threw out old conceptions of school discipline and never forced her students to sit still and do what they were told. However, the environment she created was not entirely without rules and expectations. As she explained, "The task of the educator lies in seeing that the child does not confound good with immobility and evil with activity as often happens in the case of the old-time disciplines. Our aim is to discipline for activity, for work, for good; not for immobility, not for passivity, not for obedience."[26]

Her goal was to make the children independent, to teach them to do things for themselves. She was convinced that the only valuable education was self-education; she herself was a product of that theory. The ultimate end of education, she believed, was to be in control of one's self. She saw this in the child tracing the forms of letters over and over until he suddenly realized he could write them himself. "To the casual onlooker the child seems to be learning exactitude and grace of action, to be refining his senses, to be learning how to read and write; but much more profoundly he is learning how to become his own master, how to be a man of prompt and resolute will."[27]

When children were allowed to explore and discover of their own volition, rather than being trained and forced, the learning came faster, stayed with them longer, and was much more meaningful. Maria shared the profound experience of children learning how to write themselves, after learning the sounds of all the letters of the alphabet, combining them into syllables and then words, and repeatedly following the shapes of paper letters until they could reproduce them themselves:

One beautiful December day…I went up on the roof with the children. They were playing freely about, and a number of them were gathered about me. I was sitting near a chimney, and said to a little five-year-old boy who sat beside me, "Draw me a picture of this chimney," giving him as I spoke a piece of chalk. He got down obediently and made a rough sketch of the chimney on the tiles which formed the floor of this roof terrace.…I encouraged him, praising his work. The child looked at me, smiled, remained for a moment as if on the point of bursting into some joyous act, and then cried out, "I can write! I can write!" and kneeling down again he wrote on the pavement *mano* (hand). Then, full of enthusiasm, he wrote also *camino* (chimney), *tetto* (roof). As he wrote, he continued to cry out, "I can write! I can write!" His cries of joy brought the other children, who formed a circle about him, looking down at his work in stupefied amazement. Two or three of them said to me, trembling with excitement, "Give me the chalk. I can write too." And indeed they began to write various words....

After the first word, the children, with a kind of frenzied joy, continued to write everywhere. I saw children crowding about one another at the blackboard, and behind the little ones who were standing on the floor another line would form consisting of children mounted upon chairs, so that they might write above the heads of the little ones. In a fury at being thwarted, other children, in order to find a little place where they might write, overturned the chairs upon which their companions were mounted. Others ran toward the window shutters or the door, covering them with writing. In these first days we walked upon a carpet of written signs. Daily reports showed us that the same thing was going on at home, and some of the mothers, in order to save their floors, and even the crust of their loaves upon which they found words written, gave their children presents of paper and pencil. One of these children brought to me one day a little notebook entirely filled with writing, and the mother told me that the child had written all day long and all evening, and had gone to sleep in his bed with the paper and pencil in his hand.[28]

The children experienced a similar breakthrough with reading (which, interestingly, Maria believed should come after writing). As her successes grew and were publicized, Maria attracted a group of devoted followers. She began traveling to lecture on her methods and to train teachers to apply them. A number of Montessori schools began cropping up in Italy. The wives of government ministers and aristocrats began organizing classes in their homes. She applied the same principles she had learned working with mentally handicapped and impoverished children to advantaged children, with the same results.

In October 1911, another home was established for forty-five six-year-old children from a dirty, disease-ridden Rome ghetto. Maria was again asked to be the director and again achieved the same success as she had experienced with the children in the San Lorenzo district. Anne E. George, an American teacher who had traveled to Rome to tutor under Maria, wrote of "the life, the joy, the individual independence which [she] saw in the children themselves and in everything they did." According to her, "During the year spent there these little waifs of the Ghetto had found that personal liberty and self-control that alone make it possible for any human being to do his best work and to adapt himself to the conditions of the life about him."[29]

Mrs. George toured with Maria to visit other classrooms and observed:

> Whenever we entered a classroom, I distinctly felt that a new and sweeter spirit pervaded the place, and that the children were, in an indescribable way, set free. Yet there was order in everything. With a straightforwardness stripped entirely of words, Maria Montessori taught, or to use her own word,

"directed," her children. She treated the children not as automatons, but as individual human beings. She never forced her personality or her will upon them, and made none of the efforts to attract and interest which I had often made use of.[30]

Press reports of Maria's success spread to a number of other countries, including England and the United States. Teachers from America and elsewhere began arriving in Rome in droves to learn her methods. The system was introduced in schools as far away as Australia, Argentina, and Russia. An American edition of her book, *The Montessori Method*, was published in 1912 and quickly became a bestseller.

In 1914, at the age of forty, Maria gave up all other work to devote herself to what was quickly becoming a global movement. Her focus was on training other teachers and spreading her ideas, or as E. M. Standing put it:

...the task of keeping in touch with these various movements, of guiding this vast wave of international enthusiasm, and of keeping it true to her principles....She felt increasingly the burden of a responsibility that could not be evaded. Her mission in life was now no longer a vague sense of something to come: it had crystallized out. Into her hands, without her seeking it, had been placed a key which would unlock immense treasures for humanity....She felt the duty of going forth as an apostle on behalf of all the children in the world, born and as yet unborn, to preach for their rights and liberation.[31]

She was invited by government officials, educational societies, and other interested groups to give lectures or training courses all over the world. Many people urged her to travel to America and give courses there. One night she had an unusually vivid dream where she saw herself in a rowboat on the Atlantic Ocean, making her way to America. The next morning a stranger, a representative of Mr. McClure, the owner of *McClure's Magazine*, called her with an almost irresistible offer. Mr. McClure offered to build her an institution based on her ideas and methods. Money was no object. Initially, Maria was ecstatic. In fact, she spent several days enthusiastically working out plans for the new building and the organization of the institution.

But then, suddenly, she abandoned the idea and declined the offer. As intriguing as the offer was, Maria didn't want to be tied to one continent and institution, fearing it would limit the international scope of her work. Her disciple, Anna Maccheroni said, "That was the only occasion when I have seen her depressed."[32]

WAVEMAKER WISDOM

All leaders are given "tests, trials, and traps" to try their resolve throughout their journey. These often come in the form of seemingly irresistible offers that, on the surface, would appear to hasten the work but would in fact hinder and limit it. Recognizing them takes wisdom and intuition; conquering them takes courage and commitment.

Are you recognizing your tests, trials, and traps? What are you doing to overcome them?

As it turned out, Maria did travel to America soon after to give a course at the request of the National Educational Association. There she met with Thomas Edison, a long-time admirer of her work, in his home. Soon, an American Montessori Society was formed by one Miss Helen Parkhurst, who would become her most trusted protégée; Alexander Graham Bell; and Miss Margaret Wilson, the daughter of President Woodrow Wilson. Maria Montessori became a household name in America.

Despite her well-publicized success, the Montessori movement was hampered by Maria's unwillingness and inability to train other leaders to spread and develop her work. She would not allow other teachers, even those trained by her, to train other teachers; that task she reserved for herself. She imposed strict regulations on societies that wanted to spread her method. She did not want any writings about her work published unless she checked them first and approved their contents. She insisted that her system must be used as a whole package or not at all.

She left Helen Parkhurst in charge of the main society in America. But soon after she returned to Italy, the society was fractured by petty jealousies, politics, and quarrels over money. The result left America with no authorized Montessori society, and without her express authorization, no one could teach, publicize the movement, or organize local groups.

When she was almost fifty, Maria lamented:

> I don't know what to do. There is so much of it, and nobody will ever collaborate. Either they accept what I say, and ask for more, or else they waste precious time in criticizing. What I want now is a body of colleagues, research workers, who will examine what I have already done, apply my principles as far as I have gone, not in a spirit of opposition or conviction, but as a matter of pure experiment. Then they can help me with constructive criticism, after, not before, the event. I have never yet had anyone—starting from my one previous body of knowledge—work shoulder to shoulder with me in scientific independence. Now that doctors and psychologists are beginning to take an interest in normal children, perhaps some of them will be helping me. At present I am in a kind of isolation, which is the last thing I desire.[33]

The truth is that Maria had plenty of disciples she could have developed as colleagues but failed to do so. One of her disciples, Catherine Collins, later recalled:

She was too anxious to make sure her ideas took hold to make sure of the people doing it....Her mind was always on the cause. She had to direct things herself. She would tolerate anyone who would carry out her work in her way...but over and over again she broke with those who tried to do things a different way or carry out her ideas on their own in another direction.[34]

WAVEMAKER WISDOM

Being a true leader isn't about creating an army of devoted disciples; it's about building other leaders. As John Maxwell said, "Any leader who has only followers around him will be called to continually draw on his own resources to get things done. Without other leaders to carry the load, he will become fatigued and burn out."

In their book, *Launching a Leadership Revolution*, Orrin Woodward and Chris Brady detail five levels of leadership. Level Four Leadership is developing leaders. Level Five Leadership is developing leaders who develop other leaders. Leading from these levels is the only way to create a genuine movement that spreads far beyond the original founders. By duplicating yourself, you spread your impact and deepen it exponentially.[35]

Are you creating followers or developing leaders?

The dissolution of the movement in America was soon followed by harsh criticism from establishment thinkers in education. Although her methods were embraced by Europe, it took decades for the seeds she had planted in America to fully take root and blossom.

Despite her failure to develop other leaders to continue her work, one of Maria's virtues was never wasting energy or time responding to criticism. She knew her mission and devoted herself to accomplishing it with laser focus. When a well-known professor publicly attacked her methods, she was asked why she didn't respond. She answered, "If I am going up a ladder and a dog begins to bite at my ankles, I can do one of two things—either turn round and kick out at it, or simply go on up the ladder. I prefer to go up the ladder!"[36] When she was shown a copy of a published critique of her method written by the influential academic William Kilpatrick, "in which her doctrines were proved by the writer, with chapter and verse, to be psychologically heretical," Maria said her only response was "to suggest that he should open his eyes. I can't help it if things he says are impossible continually happen."[37]

Maria persisted in her work, and history has proven its value. Today there are about 4,500 Montessori schools in America and about 20,000 worldwide, according to estimates by the North American Montessori Teacher's Association.[38] Millions of children have been helped by her method.

Whatever the specific tenets of her method, the real legacy left by Montessori was her advocacy for the rights and dignity of children. As she declared in a speech:

> The adult must understand the meaning of the moral defense of humanity, not the armed defense of nations. He must realize that the child will be the creator of the new world peace. In a suitable environment the child reveals unsuspected social characteristics. The qualities he shows will be the salvation of the world, showing us all the road to peace.

Furthermore, she shifted the educational paradigm from "filling the pail" of empty minds to "lighting the fire" of vibrant souls, to paraphrase William Butler Yeats. As Maria said, "It is not the duty of the adult to develop the child; it is his duty to safeguard the child's development."

She summed up her work and the movement connected with her name as:

> an active social campaign to make the child understood. For a multitude of weak creatures living amongst the strong, without being understood, must be an abyss of unsuspected evil. [My work is] an effort to bring about the great social revolution on behalf of the "forgotten citizen" whose rights have hitherto never been properly recognized by society.[39]

CHAPTER FOUR

CRUSADER FOR AIR POWER

*Nothing in this world can take the place of persistence.
Talent will not; nothing is more common than
unsuccessful men with talent. Genius will not;
unrewarded genius is almost a proverb. Education
will not; the world is full of educated derelicts.
Persistence and determination alone are omnipotent.*

—CALVIN COOLIDGE

"For some years, I have been afflicted with the belief that flight is possible to man. My disease has increased in severity and I feel that it will soon cost me an increased amount of money if not my life." Three years after Wilbur Wright wrote those words, and after several years of experimenting with unpowered gliders, he and his brother Orville turned their belief into reality in Kill Devil Hills, North Carolina.

On December 17, 1903, at 10:35 a.m., Orville strapped himself into their first engine-powered aircraft. Wilbur fired up the engine, and Orville headed down their make-shift runway, lifted ten feet off the ground, and flew 120 feet in twelve seconds at a speed of 6.8 miles per hour. Wilbur took a turn and flew 175 feet, after which Orville took another turn and covered 200 feet.

Orville documented their final flight of the day:

Wilbur started the fourth and last flight at just about 12 o'clock. The first few hundred feet were up and down, as before, but by the time three hundred ft had been covered, the machine was under much better control. The course for the next four or five hundred feet had but little undulation. However, when out about eight hundred feet the machine began pitching again, and, in one of its darts down-ward, struck the ground. The distance over the ground was measured to be 852 feet; the time of the flight was 59 seconds.

The brothers walked four miles to Kitty Hawk to send a telegram to their father, wherein they instructed him to inform the press. Strangely, the news failed to excite any interest. The brothers spent the next few years trying to generate interest in commercial sales of a powered aircraft, with very little success. It wasn't until 1908 that the Wright brothers signed a contract with the US Army for the purchase of an aircraft that could travel with a pilot at a speed of forty miles per hour.

But the Wright brothers were not the only aeronautical pioneers, nor were they the only ones who struggled to generate interest in the possibilities of flight.

William "Billy" Mitchell was twenty-three years old and a private in the US Army Signal Corps when Orville Wright lifted off the ground in his history-making first flight. Just three years later, while an instructor at the Army Signal School in Fort Leavenworth, Kansas, in 1906—long before flight had been proven commercially or militarily viable, before any commercial aircraft had even been sold—Billy predicted that future military conflicts would take place in the air, not on the ground. It wasn't for nothing that Billy was dubbed "America's Prophet of Air Power."

Billy was born into privilege in 1879. His father was a wealthy Wisconsin senator, his mother a member of the elite class. His grandfather Alexander Mitchell, a Scotsman millionaire banker and railroad king, was the wealthiest person in Wisconsin for his generation.

Billy was especially close to his mother, Harriet, and she urged him to match the family's previous achievements.

To prepare for that goal, Billy received a broad liberal arts education both at home, through private tutoring, and at Racine College of Wisconsin, an elite Episcopalian prep school. While at school, he displayed his natural energy and rambunctiousness when a school report stated that he had been in trouble for "talking before grace in the dining room, boisterous conduct at table, disorder in dormitory, and offences of that kind."[1]

After attending prep school, he enrolled at the college division of Columbian (now George Washington) University. Though he held his own as a student, he always preferred outdoor sports and rigorous activity to studying. Horses and guns consumed most of his attention, which made attending college an arduous task for him.

In April of 1898, an opportunity emerged for him to live the active life he dreamed of when the United States declared war on Spain, intervening for Cuba in their War of Independence from Spanish rule. Billy was only eighteen years old, a junior in college, but he promptly enlisted as a private in a Wisconsin volunteer signal regiment. He was disappointed when the conflict ended as quickly as it had begun just ten weeks later. However, his regiment was kept on active duty, and four months after the fighting had ended, they sailed to Cuba, where Mitchell was able to witness the ceremony of Spain's formal surrender of the island.

Four months after his arrival, Billy began seriously considering a long-term military career. When a conflict in the Philippines broke out over the Filipinos' resistance to US annexation, Billy volunteered as a signal officer and arrived on the islands in 1899. His service in the skirmish solidified his conviction that he was well-suited for military life. Yet he hesitated because army life wasn't quite as glamorous as it sounded. Though fighting could break out at any time, most of the army in the Philippines "had nothing to do except fight chickens, play poker, and drink whiskey." Billy's plans were to spend five or six years in the service, during which he would complete his formal education, and then "quit, have a home, some settled aim, business and association and try to earn [his] self respect and of [his] neighbors."[2]

But when friction between the United States and Germany increased, it became clear that the stagnation that Billy feared would not be a reality. When Congress passed the Army Act of 1901, it authorized a career force of 100,000 men, a fourfold increase over the standing army of 1897. After returning to the States in 1901, Billy accepted an appointment as first lieutenant in the career Signal Corps.

For the next ten years, Billy was happily engaged in the kind of fieldwork he enjoyed. He supervised the erection of a 1,700-mile telegraph line in Alaska. The army sent him overseas three times. He spent time at Fort Leavenworth, Kansas, the "intellectual center of the Army," as an instructor and commander, where he helped to develop and test new Signal Corps equipment.

During this time, he also met and married Caroline Stoddard, a member of a prominent Rochester, New York, family.

His service at Fort Leavenworth also gave him his first exposure to aircraft warfare, though on a small and limited scale. The Signal Corps had begun experimenting with balloons and dirigibles. In a 1906 article, Mitchell predicted:

> [The dirigible might] course at will over a battle-field, carry messages out of a besieged fortress, or sail alone above a beleaguered place, immune from the action of men on the earth's surface....By towing another balloon, loaded with explosive, several hundred pounds of guncotton could be dropped from the balloon which it is towing in the midst of the enemy's fortifications."[3]

Mitchell also thought that dirigibles might act as "scouts for the Navy to detect the presence of submarine vessels." He concluded the article with his prophetic statement that "conflicts, no doubt, will be carried on in the future in the air, on the surface of the earth and water, and under the earth and water."[4]

After his Fort Leavenworth experience, Mitchell served a two-year tour in the Philippines, consisting of under-cover reconnaissance of Japanese activities in the islands between Formosa and the Philippines. When he returned to the States, Billy reported that war with Japan was inevitable and urged the army to prepare.

His report garnered attention, and he was asked to take a general staff assignment in Washington. He accepted on the grounds that it would further his career by helping him develop political and social contacts. At the age of thirty-four, Billy was fully committed to a military career. In his staff assignment, he became increasingly interested and influential in general military policy. His technological background made him realize that the United States was increasingly vulnerable, "as exemplified in transport methods and means which daily bring us closer to prospective enemies."[5]

When war broke out in Europe, Billy began publishing reports urging the army to increase its conflict readiness. Included in his reports, at the request of President Wilson, was a survey of America's aviation needs—one of the earliest comprehensive statements on American military aviation policy.

But the office work in his general staff position had worn on Billy, and he longed to return to active field service. In June 1916, he accepted an assignment with the Corps' Aviation Section. By July, he had won a promotion to major and was given the responsibility to build up army aviation, including the task of stepping up flight training. By fall of that year, he began pilot training himself in his off-duty time at the Curtiss Aviation School in Newport News, Virginia.

His flight time paid off when the War Department decided to send an officer to Europe as an aeronautical observer. Mitchell got the job on the basis of his personal flying knowledge and left for France on March 19, 1917. Two weeks later, President Wilson asked Congress to declare war on Germany.

By taking initiative—seeing what needs to happen and acting on your own without being asked—you find that opportunities are created and doors are opened. As Tony Robbins said, "Success comes from taking the initiative and following up, persisting…. What simple action could you take today to produce a new momentum toward success in your life?"

How can you take more initiative? Where do you see need, and what can and should you do about it?

After arriving in Paris, Mitchell set up an office using his own money. He immediately took an intensive course in aeronautics taught by the top Allied airmen. He was stunned to learn how much more advanced flight was in Europe than in the States. Of course, the war had necessitated the advancement. In 1914, the best European planes flew at sixty-five miles per hour for a range of about 200 miles. After three years of warfare, however, fleets included both fighters and bombers, with their best fighter planes approaching 120 miles per hour and bombers flying at eighty-five miles per hour. US planes at the time were only comparable to the 1914 European models.

The role of aviation, as it had moved from simple observation by single aircraft to complex strategies involving hundreds of planes, had changed the face of the war. Control of the airspace above the front was now required for a force to be able to operate with full freedom on the ground.

Billy's understanding of the new need for air power increased as he developed a relationship with Major General Hugh Trenchard of the British Royal Flying Corps. Under Trenchard's leadership, the RFC had become a force to be reckoned with, far superior to the air force of any other European nation. Trenchard was known for pushing the boundaries of established theory. Whereas most commanders saw the role of airplanes as simply hovering over ground force positions to protect them from aerial observation and attack, Trenchard pushed for "relentless and incessant offensive."[6]

After meeting with Allied airmen and commanders, Mitchell urged the army to create an American air force, consisting of 4,300 bombers and fighters, to assist the Allies in their offensive approach. But Washington authorities did not view Mitchell as an expert, and they were still steeped in the old idea that air power was primarily for reconnaissance. Little attention was paid to Mitchell's frantic demands.

When Major General John Pershing arrived in Paris in June of 1917, he made Mitchell the aviation officer of the American Expeditionary Force. Mitchell promptly requested the general's approval for a "tactical" and "strategical" aviation force, based on what he'd learned from Allied airmen. He stressed that "no decision on the ground would be reached before a decision in the air" and told Pershing, perhaps rashly, that strategic aviation could have "a greater influence on the ultimate decision of the war than any other arm."[7]

Pershing referred Mitchell's recommendations to a board of officers, including Mitchell, and instructed them to produce a "complete aviation project for the U.S. Army in France."[8] The panel endorsed Mitchell's proposal, but Pershing, cautiously feeling his way through a situation that no American commander had ever faced, ignored the question of strategic aviation for several months. It would take a year for President Wilson to finally order that the Air Service be separated from the Signal Corps, a small but important step toward building a strategic air force.

Political wrangling, vast differences of opinion, organizational confusion, and justifiable cautiousness made for slow progress for the Air Service. The French urged the Americans to help them build and supply an aviation program. When Mitchell was made a colonel in September 1917, his influence within the budding program grew. But progress was agonizingly slow for his driven personality.

Pershing finally put the first squadron into fighting in early April of 1918, with Mitchell being, loosely, the commander of the force. Billy saw a hint of the future when he was finally able to coordinate a fleet of two hundred French and American bombers, which dropped 39 tons of bombs, followed by British units dropping 40 more tons in the same twenty-four-hour period, on German troops. The 79-ton total in twenty-four hours was impressive compared to the total of 138 tons dropped during the entire war.

But the armistice signed on November 11, 1918, prevented Billy from experimenting further. He was ordered to return to the States. A naval officer who returned home from England with Mitchell noted that he "was fully prepared with evidence, plans, data, propaganda posters and articles, to break things open for air power as the sole requisite of the national defense in the future."[9] When Billy arrived home in March 1919, he was determined to bring about a revolution in American military policy. Although air power had not proven to be decisive in the war itself, Mitchell knew that its development presented ominous implications for the future. His ambitious plans included elevating aeronautics to a separate military division, as an equal partner with the army and navy—a radical idea at the time.

Initially, he had been appointed as Director of Military Aeronautics, but when he reported for duty, he found that the post had been eliminated due to postwar reorganization. He was placed instead in the Air Service as Third Assistant Executive and Chief, where he would have tactical supervision.

But once again, Mitchell would have to be patient. Under President Warren Harding, the military was rapidly demobilized. The number of Air Service officers plummeted from 20,000 to little more than 200 virtually overnight. Both military and commercial aviation were still novelties, though a few informed congressmen recognized the need for aviation in national defense. The debate revolved around where, how much, and under whose control it should be.

Mitchell pushed hard, wielding influence where he could to persuade commanders and policymakers that aerial warfare was now as important as naval and ground warfare. Technology, he asserted, had shattered the old framework of military policy. Though he recognized that his proposals were "drastic" and required "a great deal of discussion," Billy was optimistic that reason would win the day. Like all crusaders, his ideas seemed to him to be self-evident and therefore incontrovertible.[10]

Unfortunately, Billy was largely alone in his views. Most military experts, ranging from Major General Pershing to almost every general officer and admiral, were against him. As the saying goes, "Nothing is so firmly lodged as the ignorance of experts." The army's leadership built a comprehensive case against Billy's ideas. The Assistant Secretary of the Navy, Franklin D. Roosevelt, was the first government official to publicly attack Billy's ideas, dismissing his views as "pernicious" and declaring that aviation was but a servant of the navy. One month later, the Division of Naval Aeronautics was disbanded, leaving naval aviation with no definite status within its own service.[11]

The central question debated by all leaders was: Can aviation independently effect a decision in war? Fierce debate naturally arose over which service would be responsible for coordinating the activities of an aviation division. Billy's essential answer to his critics was to look to the future. Aviation was still in its infancy, he knew, but as the technology developed, it would need to play a more prominent role, and room would need to be made for it within the military.

During 1919, eight different measures were introduced in Congress to establish a Department of Aeronautics. All of them were defeated. Billy and his supporters gained a tiny bit of ground with the passage of the National Defense Act of 1920, which officially established the Army Air Service, a combat arm with 1,516 officers and 16,000 enlisted men in an overall army of 280,000.[12]

Mitchell was left with two options: (1) continue pushing for the development of aviation on any front open to him and (2) appeal to public opinion. Under Mitchell's leadership, the Air Service sponsored the first air race in the United States, which helped focus congressional attention on aviation. He pushed for the establishment of an airways system for coordinating all aeronautical activity over the country. In July 1920, the Air Service made the first flight from New York to Nome, Alaska—a 9,000-mile trip. Mitchell was always driving, always demanding new innovation and higher standards of excellence. As one aviation pioneer said of him, "No one could be content in his presence."[13]

Billy devised a complete tactical plan—the first of its kind—for a defense against enemy fleets, concluding his analysis by saying that "an attack carried out" according to his plan would "render surface craft incapable of operating to the same extent that they have heretofore, if it does not entirely drive them off the surface of the water."[14] During a congressional hearing a few days later, he challenged Congress to test his claims.

Meanwhile, Billy became a skillful and effective publicity hound, garnering attention-grabbing headlines in the *New York Times* and publishing articles in a number of national magazines.

In November 1920, the navy finally agreed to perform tests and invited Mitchell to see the results. The tests were performed in secret on the battleship *Indiana*. Bombs were positioned in key points on and near the ship and then exploded, with only dummy bombs being dropped from the air. This was hardly the test Billy had envisioned, but it was a start. The damage inflicted justified further aerial tests.

By January 1921, thanks largely to Mitchell's relentless media campaign, public pressure had become intense for a bombing test to be performed by the Air Service. An editorial in the *New York Times*, for example, opined that the nation could not afford to ignore Mitchell's claims. By the end of the month, two congressmen had introduced resolutions in the House and Senate ordering the navy to give Mitchell the necessary resources for a test. A triumphant Mitchell crowed, "We are going to smoke these people out that do not believe in the air business and make them 'either fish or cut bait.'"[15]

While waiting for the tests, Billy published his first book, *Our Air Force*, that spring, giving his readers an authoritative picture of aviation's progress.

On July 22, after a frustrating political battle, Mitchell finally got the chance he'd been waiting for. The navy provided him with an obsolete German battleship, the *Ostfriesland*, on which to test his theories. His crews dropped six 2,000-pound bombs on the battleship. Within twenty-one minutes, the ship plunged toward the bottom of the sea. Though the navy refuted the test on a few technicalities, the fact was that Billy had sunk a battleship, as he had claimed he could, and the public was deeply impressed. The Joint Board evaluated the test and recognized that "aircraft carrying high-capacity, high-explosive

Ex-German battleship *Ostfriesland* takes a blow from a 2,000-lb. aerial bomb. Minutes later, the target ship sank by the stern.

bombs of sufficient size have adequate offensive power to sink or seriously damage any naval vessel at present constructed, provided such projectiles can be placed in the water alongside the vessel."[16]

Though the report should have been a major coup for the embattled Mitchell, he was not pleased with the board's less than urgent recommendations of what to do about it. The report called for developing aviation, adding aircraft carriers to the navy, and improving antiaircraft armament. But the board also viewed aviation as only adding "to the complexity of naval warfare" instead of solving the problems it presented.[17]

Impatient, Billy took matters into his own hands and leaked his own report to the press, asserting that a fundamental change in national defense policy was needed. The end result, he wrote, would be a "Department of National Defense...with a staff common to all the services" and with "subsecretaries for the Army, Navy, and the Air Force." When the "bombshell" report, as he called it, incited fierce conflict within the Air Service, followed by the collapse of his sixteen-year marriage with Caroline, the battle-weary Mitchell left the scene of controversy and sailed to Europe. He was assigned to study European aeronautical progress, as well as Air Service operations and the American defense system in the Pacific.[18]

When Billy returned to the States in the fall of 1922, he discovered that his rival, General Patrick, had taken over the Air Service, thus limiting his activities and influence. But he still found ways to gain ground. In November

1922, for example, he broke the world speed record in an airplane, which won him international attention. He still wrote for the press, but Secretary of War John Weeks silenced him on controversial topics by requiring that he submit all articles for official clearance before they were allowed to be published.

Billy took a break from the political battles and resigned himself to fighting from within by doing everything he could to develop aviation. He pushed for increased efficiency within the Air Service. He presented his men with various tactical problems and had them perform drills for each, after which he gave them thorough performance evaluations. And he developed a manual on bombardment.

But his tests were stymied by the poor condition of the Air Service, which had noticeably deteriorated between 1920 and 1923. A commissioned board observed that "unless steps are taken to improve conditions in the Air Service it will in effect be practically demobilized at an early date." But Congress only appropriated less than half of the $26 million budget proposed by General Patrick. When Warren Harding died prematurely, Calvin Coolidge took office, and his rigid economy in government did not bode well for further aviation improvement.[19]

Billy was remarried in October 1923 to Elizabeth Trumbull. After the wedding, he and Elizabeth left on a honeymoon through the Pacific that would double as an inspection by Mitchell of the American security position in that area. When he returned home in July 1924, after visits to the Hawaiian and Philippine Islands, India, China,

Manchuria, Korea, and Japan, he submitted a 325-page report detailing the same conclusions he had arrived at in 1909–1911: War between the United States and Japan was inevitable. Japan was the dominant nation in Asia and was prepared to undertake such a war. America's strength was so great, Mitchell said, that the Japanese could only hope to defeat it by using the most advanced methods possible. Of course, for him these methods centered on aviation. Though it would take years for technology to catch up with his theories, Billy had essentially predicted the Japanese attack on Pearl Harbor almost two decades before it happened.

After his Pacific trip, in the fall of 1924, Billy made one more effort to push for his goal of an independent and advanced air force, operating under the conviction that "changes in military systems are brought about only through the pressure of public opinion or disaster in war."[20] This last campaign would eventually result in the end of his military career.

Acting as the personal representative of President Coolidge, he began the campaign with a daring speech to delegates of the National Aeronautics Convention, wherein he divulged his long-hidden ideas on strategic bombardment. Following the speech, and in direct defiance of the directive issued by Secretary Weeks to submit all articles for official approval, he sent five bold articles to the *Saturday Evening Post*. Collectively, the articles were seen as a broadside to everyone within the ranks who disagreed with him.

Unfortunately, as his publicity campaign continued, Mitchell damaged his credibility with increasingly sensational claims and reckless statements that could not be proven in an attempt to hold his place in the headlines. The defiant campaign revealed his greatest weakness—flamboyant egoism—and quickly became a classic case of the ends justifying the means. As biographer Alfred Hurley wrote:

> [Mitchell] erred in believing that the realization of his vision would justify his tactics. Those tactics included his denial of the integrity of an often equally dedicated opposition, his substitution of promises for performance, and his failure to sustain the kind of day-to-day self-effacing effort that builds any institution, whether military or otherwise."[21]

WAVEMAKER WISDOM

In striving for worthy goals and fighting justified battles, never lose your integrity or erode your credibility. Keep your ego in check with constant self-assessment. Don't deceive yourself into justifying questionable means for any end, however admirable.

Are you fighting for the right reasons? Are you keeping your ego in check and being absolutely honest with yourself in your tactics?

There was more than a little truth in Secretary Weeks's statement declaring that Mitchell's "whole course had been so lawless, so contrary to the building up of an efficient organization, so lacking in reasonable teamwork, so indicative of a personal desire for publicity at the expense of everyone with whom he associated that his actions render him unfit for a high administrative post such as he now occupies."[22] On the other hand, such a statement was to be expected from a deeply-entrenched opponent.

Despite the professional antagonism, army, navy, and political leadership knew that there was truth to Mitchell's claims and merit in his goals. General Patrick submitted a plan to the War Department calling for the creation of an Army Air Corps, similar to the semi-independent Marine Corps. President Coolidge began following the matter with great interest.

In August 1925, Mitchell published another book, *Winged Defense: The Development and Possibilities of Modern Air Power*, which would become his most famous, though it was a "hastily compiled collection" of previously published articles and statements before Congress.[23]

When the dirigible *Shenandoah* crashed after running into severe weather over Ohio, Mitchell seized the opportunity to launch his most controversial offensive to date. He gave reporters a written nine-page statement that blasted the "incompetency, criminal negligence, and almost treasonable administration of the national defense by the Navy and War Departments." Four days later, he told reporters, "Let every American know that we are going to better our

National Defense, that we are on the warpath and that we are going to stay there until these conditions are remedied."[24] Secretly, he confided in letters to Elizabeth, "Now people will buy our books and writings," thus betraying at least partial inauthenticity.[25]

Two weeks later, the War Department, on the direct order of President Coolidge, announced its decision to court-martial Mitchell, accusing him of violating the 96th Article of War, an omnibus article that Mitchell's chief counsel, Congressman Frank Reid, declared to be unconstitutional as a violation of free speech. The court-martial began in early November and lasted for seven weeks.

During the proceedings, Mitchell kept up his media campaign. In one radio address, he told his listeners:

> For centuries we have been accustomed to entrust the national defense to armies and navies and sometimes to regard them more as institutions than as agencies of the people for protecting the country from all enemies, both without and within. So long have these agencies been supreme in their particular field that any change from the ancient and fixed systems of an army on the land and a fleet in the sea [has] been looked on with real alarm and misgiving by these forces. The traditional military mind is notoriously sensitive to any breath of criticism, and any attempt to tear away the veil of its mystery is apt to be greeted by the cry of sacrilege.[26]

He warned that future wars would be won by aircraft striking at the enemy's centers of industry and declared:

> It is therefore impossible for people to put their trust in armies or navies alone. Airpower must be given a place of equal importance. It must not be muzzled, gagged, or belittled. By burrowing our heads in the sand on the advice of our armies and navies, we cannot escape the danger of airpower by shutting it out of our sight.
>
> We have brought these matters to the attention of the American people as it has been impossible in this country through our existing governmental agencies to organize our defense in a modern manner in accordance with the methods of our present civilization. We want every American to take a patriotic interest in these matters which concern us all.[27]

The seven weeks of the trial were long and tedious. Many military leaders, including some of the judges, were not happy with the proceedings. Major General Douglas MacArthur, the youngest of the twelve judges, summed it up when he described the order to sit on Mitchell's court-martial as "one of the most distasteful orders I ever received."[28] Privately, though most of them found Mitchell's conduct unbecoming of an officer, they respected his quest and agreed that changes needed to be made. Public opinion was also in favor of Mitchell, thanks to his aggressive and persistent media campaigns.

Still, on December 17, 1925, they found him guilty of conduct prejudicial to "good order and military discipline [and]…conduct of a nature to bring discredit upon the military service."[29] Billy's unprecedented sentence was five years' suspension from active duty without pay or allowances. He was also denied claim to retirement benefits.

A willing martyr, Mitchell regarded his trial as a "necessary cog in the wheel of progress, a requisite step in the modernization and rehabilitation of the national defense of the country."[30] There was truth to his remarks. Whatever might be said of his campaign, he had forced the administration to consider aviation much more seriously than it ever had. Progress, however slow, was being made, due in large part to Mitchell's efforts.

Though his influence had been injured, and though he could only speak from the sidelines, Billy was not even remotely finished with his crusade. Freed from any official constraint, he began speaking out and publishing with more vigor than ever. Within the next two years, more than ten million subscribers read his ideas in such publications as Liberty, the Saturday Evening Post, Colliers, Outlook, Atlantic Monthly, and the Annals of the American Academy of Political and Social Science.

WAVEMAKER WISDOM

Every time you're knocked down, pick yourself up off the mat. As Winston Churchill said, "Never give in—never, never, never, never, in nothing great or small, large or petty, never give in except to convictions of honour and good sense. Never yield to force; never yield to the apparently overwhelming might of the enemy."

How can you motivate yourself to keep striving and fighting? How can apparent setbacks actually be used as new freedoms to continue your quest?

With the goal of changing public opinion, Mitchell also created the United Air Force Association, an organization dedicated to the creation of an independent air force service in the military with the mission of strategic bombardment. When Charles Lindbergh made history flying from New York to Paris, public interest was spurred, and at long last, American aviation seemed to be on its way.

In 1932 (as if Great Depression–ridden American citizens didn't have enough to worry about), Mitchell published his most sensationalized articles warning of an impending conflict with Japan: "Are We Ready for War with Japan?" and "Will Japan Try to Conquer the United States?"

The years 1933 to 1935 were hard for Billy. The full effect of the Depression impacted him financially. President

Roosevelt remained noncommittal about Mitchell's national defense goals. The army still asserted that aviation belonged under its control. In an appearance before a congressional commission in 1935, Billy suddenly found himself alone in his insistence on a separate service; his allies had wearied of the struggle. Billy admitted to a friend that the road to success was "long and tortuous."[31]

He became increasingly belligerent and suffered accordingly in his social and political contacts. In January 1936, the long, tough battle caught up with him, and he fell ill with influenza, complicated by heart trouble. On the same day that he admitted himself to the hospital, the House Military Affairs Committee considered a bill to restore him to the retired list as a colonel. But the proposal was voted down; though they recognized his service to the nation, the committee members did not want to appear to approve of his methods. That final disappointment may have been more than Billy could endure. His illness took a turn for the worse, and he died on February 17, 1936.

Less than six years after his death, the American people were shocked to discover just how prophetic Mitchell's predictions were when Japan attacked Pearl Harbor on Sunday, December 7, 1941. Another of his predictions came true when Japan finally collapsed under a combined American air and submarine offensive. In Europe, the Nazi aeronautical offensive also confirmed Billy's predictions. World War II proved air power to be indispensable. As General Douglas MacArthur wrote, "Had [Mitchell]

lived through World War II, he would have seen the fulfill-
ment of many of his prophecies of air warfare."

So what place should Billy Mitchell have in history?
Biographer Douglas Waller writes:

> Mitchell could be vain, egotistical, power hungry,
> and a self-promoter. He was outspoken when he
> should have been prudent, opinionated when he
> should have been objective, confrontational when
> he should have been accommodating, self-centered
> when he should have been a team player. He saw
> evil in many who simply had honest disagreements
> with him, made enemies of men who could have
> been valuable allies.[32]

But in defense of Mitchell, Waller continues, "Great
leaders, particularly those in wartime, have outsized
egos. Institutional mavericks, whistle-blowers, critics who
press for reform in bureaucracies all tend to be abrasive,
outspoken, hard to get along with. Prophets by nature are
opinionated and overconfident."[33]

Whatever we can learn from Mitchell's personal fail-
ings, we can learn more from his strengths and contributions. He knew exactly what needed to happen, and he
drove relentlessly to achieve that goal. He had the courage
of his convictions. America's military progress would
undoubtedly have been much slower had Billy not pushed
for reform.

Mitchell's predictions were exonerated, and his objectives were achieved. The United States Air Force was

formed as a separate branch of the military on September 18, 1947, under the National Security Act of 1947. As of 2012, the independent US Air Force operates 5,551 aircraft, 450 ICBMs, and 63 satellites. It has a $140 billion budget with 332,854 active personnel, 185,522 civilian personnel, 71,400 reserve personnel, and 106,700 air guard personnel.

In 1942, President Franklin D. Roosevelt recognized Mitchell's contributions to air power and elevated him to the rank of major general on the Army Air Corps retired list and petitioned Congress to posthumously award him the Congressional Gold Medal, "in recognition of his outstanding pioneer service and foresight in the field of American military aviation." We've come a long way since Orville and Wilbur Wright's makeshift aircraft, and we can thank Wavemaker Billy Mitchell for much of our aeronautical progress.

CHAPTER FIVE

A RIPPLE CAUSED BY AN ORDINARY SUNDAY SCHOOL TEACHER

The men who followed Him were unique in their generation. They turned the world upside down because their hearts had been turned right side up. The world has never been the same.

—EVANGELIST BILLY GRAHAM

On November 7, 2013, a man who had grown up on a family dairy farm and gone on to became a preacher who counseled with kings, queens, presidents, and celebrities was wheeled into his ninety-fifth birthday celebration, where he preached his final sermon via a prerecorded video, declaring that "[America] is in great need of a spiritual awakening. There have been times that I've wept as I've gone from city to city and I've seen how far people have wandered from God." After having preached in his lifetime to more people (2.2 billion) than any Protestant in history and having appeared on Gallup's list of the "Ten Most Admired Men in the World" fifty-six times since 1955, more than any individual on the planet,[1] he delivered his final testimony to the world, affirming that "there is no other way of salvation except through the cross of Christ."[2]

That man was Billy Graham, the evangelical Christian preacher who declared, "My one purpose in life is to help people find a personal relationship with God, which, I believe, comes through knowing Christ," and who took Christ literally when He said in Mark 16:15 (KJV), "Go ye into all the world, and preach the gospel to every creature." According to his staff, more than 3.2 million people have responded to the invitation at Billy Graham Crusades to "accept Jesus Christ as their personal Savior."

Graham has preached on every continent, from remote African villages to major cities, including a crusade at Madison Square Garden in New York City that ran for sixteen weeks. Those to whom he has ministered have ranged from heads of state to the simple-living bushmen of Australia and the wandering tribes of Africa and the Middle East. He has conducted preaching missions in virtually every country of the former Eastern bloc, including the former Soviet Union. He has published thirty-one books throughout his lifetime, including *The Jesus Generation* in 1971, which sold 200,000 copies in the first two weeks; *Angels: God's Secret Agents* in 1975, which sold one million copies within ninety days; *How to Be Born Again* in 1977, which had the largest first printing in publishing history with 800,000 copies; and *Approaching Hoofbeats: The Four Horsemen of the Apocalypse* in 1983, which was listed for several weeks on the *New York Times* bestseller list.[3]

Greg Laurie, the senior pastor at the 15,000-member Harvest Christian Fellowship in Riverside, California, declared, "I'd say, without question, that Billy Graham is the greatest evangelist who has ever lived, not just in our generation, but in any generation. No one has even come close to accomplishing what he has." Bill Leonard, a Wake Forest University Divinity School professor, said Graham remains "an American phenomenon, the most enduring and perhaps the most beloved preacher in American religious history. Graham is a major historical figure, not merely to American evangelicals, but to American Christianity in general."[4]

At age ninety-five, Graham is not finished preaching the gospel. He recently launched his biggest evangelical outreach, which he hopes will lead to a much-needed revival. More than 25,000 churches—one of every twelve in America—are participating in the outreach along with 2,300 churches in Canada. He said:

> We have been going down the wrong road for a long time. Seemingly, man has learned to live without God, preoccupied and indifferent toward Him and concerned only about material security and pleasure. And yet mankind is also adrift morally and spiritually, confused and fearful because he does not know where he is or where he is going. He lives in a world dangerously torn by hate and violence and

conflict, and yet he feels powerless to do anything about them. He also knows his own heart is driven by destructive passions and motives he cannot seem to control or change.

The answer? According to Graham, people need to:

[repent of their sins, turn to God, and] take the narrow road that Jesus talks about in the Bible. The narrow road means that you forsake sin and you obey God, that you live up to the Ten Commandments and that you live up to the Sermon on the Mount, desiring to please God in everything. The narrow road is hard and it is difficult; you can't do that yourself. You need God's help, and that's the reason we ask people to come to receive Christ, because when you receive Him, the Holy Spirit comes to live within to help us live the life. Our world is desperately seeking answers to the deepest questions of life—answers that can only be found in the Gospel. That is the reason for my hope, that there can be changed hearts and a changed society as we yield ourselves to Christ.

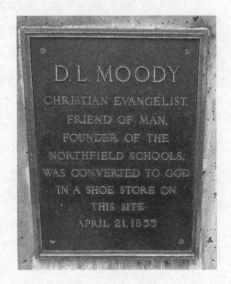

Billy Graham is a Wavemaker in his own right, whose impact will continue to be felt through generations long after he has passed. But his colossal waves are the generational result of one tiny ripple caused by an obscure Sunday school teacher, Edward Kimble, in the mid-nineteenth century. All we know of Mr. Kimble is that he was a Sunday school teacher at the Congregational Church of Mount Vernon in Boston, Massachusetts, where Dr. Edward Norris Kirk was pastor.

In 1854, a seventeen-year-old boy by the name of Dwight moved to Boston and began attending the Congregational Church. Dwight had been born into a large family. When he was four years old, his father, a small farmer and stonemason, died at the age of forty-one, leaving his mother, Betsey, to care for nine children, including newborn twins. Betsey struggled to support the family. As hard as she tried, she still had to send some of her children off, including Dwight, to work for their room and board. The family Dwight was sent to fed him nothing but cornmeal, porridge, and milk three times a day. When he complained to his mother, she brought him back home.

When Dwight turned seventeen, he moved to Boston to work. After getting rejected for jobs time and time again, he finally convinced his uncle to let him work in his shoe store. His uncle conceded with a few requirements, including that Dwight attend church. Dwight went grudgingly and showed little promise of a converted Christian.

On April 21, 1855, Edward Kimble felt prompted to visit Dwight in the shoe store and bear testimony of the gospel.

At first he vacillated, knowing Dwight's lack of enthusiasm about the gospel. But he followed the prompting and entered the store, where he found Dwight stocking shoes in the back room. Edward shared his faith and was surprised when Dwight prayed and received Jesus Christ on the spot.

WAVEMAKER WISDOM

Never, ever ignore spiritual promptings. Allow God to guide and direct your life; He knows how to use you for good better than you do with your limited perspective.

What spiritual promptings have you followed in the past? What have they led to, what doors have they opened in your life? Which ones have you ignored, and why?

Fully converted, Dwight applied for formal church membership but was disappointed when his application was rejected. As Edward Kimball later wrote:

> I can truly say, and in saying it I magnify the infinite grace of God as bestowed upon him, that I have seen few persons whose minds were spiritually darker than was his when he came into my Sunday School class; and I think that the committee of the Mount Vernon Church seldom met an applicant for membership more unlikely ever to become

a Christian of clear and decided views of Gospel truth, still less to fill any extended sphere of public usefulness.

But Dwight persisted and was received as a church member on May 4, 1856.[5]

Little did Edward Kimble know the chain of events he had sparked by following that one prompting to visit Dwight in the shoe store that day. That rough, obstinate, and "spiritually dark" shoe salesman was Dwight Lyman Moody, known as D. L. Moody, hailed as one of the greatest evangelists in the nineteenth century. In a forty-year period "he won a million souls, founded three Christian schools, launched a great Christian publishing business, established a world-renowned Christian conference center, and inspired literally thousands of preachers to win souls and conduct revivals."[6]

Soon after his conversion, feeling inspired to convert other souls, Dwight dropped his ambition to make $100,000 as a shoe salesman and began preaching the gospel. If anyone ever appeared unqualified and unlikely to be a great evangelist and preacher, it was Dwight L. Moody. He had only a sixth-grade education. He was short and weighed more than three hundred pounds. He was not charismatic in the slightest. His speech and grammar were unpolished. After hearing Dwight preach, the famous London Baptist preacher Charles Spurgeon said, "He is the only man I ever heard who said 'Mesopotamia' in one syllable." His sermons rarely lasted longer than thirty minutes and were very simple in expressing God's love for the sinner. It was said of him that "He was an evangelist sent from God, for no man could have done the ministry he accomplished, except God was with him."[7]

Edward Kimble, Dwight's old Sunday school teacher, wrote of Dwight's first attempts at preaching:

> The first meeting I ever saw him at was in a little old shanty that had been abandoned by a saloon-keeper. Mr. Moody had got the place to hold the meetings in at night. I went there a little late; and the first thing I saw was a man standing up with a few tallow candles around him, holding a negro boy, and trying to read to him the story of the Prodigal Son and a great many words he could not read out, and had to skip. I thought, "If the Lord can ever use such an instrument as that for His honor and glory, it will astonish me." As a result of his tireless labor, within a year the average attendance at his school was 650, while sixty volunteers from various churches served as teachers. It became so well known that the just-elected President Lincoln visited and spoke at a Sunday School meeting on November 25, 1860.

WAVEMAKER WISDOM

In your leadership efforts, never judge anyone based on their appearance. Remember what the Lord told Samuel in 1 Samuel 16:7 (KJV) when the young

David's impressive brother Eliab was brought before him: "Look not on his countenance, or on the height of his stature; because I have refused him: for the Lord seeth not as man seeth; for man looketh on the outward appearance, but the Lord looketh on the heart." Learn to see people as God sees them and bring out the best in them by how you treat them.

Who have you underestimated in your life? What should you do about it?

As his congregation grew, Moody needed a permanent home, so he started the Illinois Street Church in Chicago in the spring of 1871. In October, the Great Chicago Fire destroyed his church, his home, and the homes of most of his church members. His family had to flee for their lives, and as Moody later said, he saved nothing but his reputation and his Bible. His church was rebuilt within three months at a nearby location as the Chicago Avenue Church.

Moody began organizing summer conferences, which were attended by prominent Christian preachers and evangelists from around the world. In the spring of 1872, Moody traveled to England where he preached nearly a hundred times and established his reputation as a great evangelist. He routinely preached to full stadiums seating 2,000 to 4,000 people. One meeting at the Botanic Gardens Palace held between 15,000 to 30,000 people. His tour continued through 1875, with crowds of thousands at all his meetings.

He returned to the United States, where he continued preaching to crowds of 12,000 to 20,000 all across the country, from Boston and New York to San Francisco and San Diego. He inspired many missionaries to travel throughout the world preaching the gospel, including to inland China. He died of heart failure on December 22, 1899.

While D. L. Moody was on tour on England in 1872, a young preacher by the name of Frederick B. Meyer visited one of his meetings at Priory Street Baptist Chapel. Meyer felt deeply stirred by Moody's sermon, and the two preachers formed a lifelong friendship. Sparked by Moody's fervent testimony, Meyer felt inspired to embark upon his own evangelical ministry.

He preached in London for fifteen years, starting with a congregation of a hundred attendees and building it to more than 2,000. He then left on a mission to South Africa and the Far East. During his pastorship he also frequently visited the United States and Canada. At the age of eighty, he went on his twelfth American preaching campaign, traveling more than 15,000 miles and addressing more than three hundred meetings. He preached more than 16,000 sermons in his lifetime. He was well known for his outcry against social evils and was responsible for closing more than five hundred brothels. He also formed a prison aid society. He passed away in 1929.

One author wrote of him, "The phrasing of [Meyer's] sermons was simple and direct; he polished his discourses as an artist polishes a perfect stone. There was always a glowing imagery in his words; his speech was pastoral, lovely as an English valley washed in sunlight....In his day, great wars raged. Those who went to hear him forgot the battles." The London preacher Charles Spurgeon said, "Meyer preaches as a man who has seen God face to face."[8]

The ripple caused by Edward Kimble, which had become a formidable wave with D. L. Moody, continued gaining size and momentum, through Frederick Meyer and beyond.

In the summer of 1886, Frederick Meyer was on tour in the United States where he preached at a conference in Northfield, Massachusetts. A sad, confused, and discouraged young preacher, Wilbur Chapman, who had just lost his wife, was in attendance. His life—and that of millions of others—was forever altered when he heard Meyer proclaim, "If you are not willing to give up everything for Christ, are you willing to be made willing?" Chapman said of this experience, "That remark changed my whole ministry; it seemed like a new star in the sky of my life."[9]

Chapman was born into a Christian home in Richmond, Indiana, on June 17, 1859. His mother died when he was thirteen. Of the choice to follow Christ that he made in Sunday school one day at the age of seventeen, he said, "[Mrs. Binkley] put her hand under my elbow...and I stood up with the others. I do not know if this was the day of my conversion, but I do know it was the day of my acknowledgment of Christ."

He decided to enter the ministry and went to college. While studying at Lake Forest University, he had some doubts about his commitment to Christ, saying that he sometimes felt saved and sometimes not. Seeking assurance, he attended a sermon preached by D. L. Moody, where he had a private visit with Moody. He left the meeting feeling more confident and assured. He was officially ordained to the ministry on April 13, 1881.

Six days after graduating, he married his sweetheart, Irene, and the newlywed couple accepted a calling to minister to two churches. Their first child was born on April 1, 1886. Unfortunately, Irene died a month later due to complications with the birth. Wilbur was devastated. It was during this time that he heard Frederick Meyer preach; his life was changed, and he felt fully solidified in his commitment to preach the gospel.

He remarried two years later and then accepted a call to preach at Bethany Presbyterian Church of Philadelphia in January 1890. There he grew prayer meetings to over 1,000 participants. He conducted a revival and brought more than 400 new members into the church, the majority of them making professions of faith. He built the church into a strong spiritual, educational, and social center that attracted hundreds, with as many as 300 joining at one given time. As the church became nationally known, requests for his evangelistic services multiplied.

For the next few years, Chapman traveled across the country on evangelistic crusades. In 1895, D. L. Moody called him the "greatest evangelist in the country."[10]

Later that year, he returned to his church in Philadelphia, and built it into the largest church in the country, with a record-high enrollment of 6,027 in 1898. More than 16,000 converts signified professions of faith during his ministry there.

In 1905, Chapman began promoting new methods of urban mass evangelism. In his first attempt, he took seventeen evangelists to Pittsburgh, where he divided the city into districts. The whole city went into action, with some 7,000 professing salvation. In 1906, the same operation in Syracuse, New York, had similar results.

In March 1908, he led a massive revival in Philadelphia, cooperating with more than 400 churches comprising almost every denomination in the area, including Quakers, Lutherans, Episcopalians, Moravians, Mennonites, and Schwenkfelder churches. It was estimated that 35,000 people attended nightly for six weeks, for a total of 1,470,000. This surpassed the Moody Crusade of 1875–1876, when 1,050,000 were reached. Converts were estimated at 8,000. A similar campaign was completed in Boston. Through 1912, it was estimated that he had preached 50,000 sermons to some 60 million people.[11]

The Edward Kimble–catalyzed wave continued when, in 1893, Wilbur Chapman hired a young baseball player, Billy Sunday, as his "advance man" at forty dollars per week.

Billy Sunday was born into poverty in a two-room log cabin in Iowa in 1862. His father, serving in the Union Army at the time, died of pneumonia, so Billy never knew his father. When Billy was ten years old, his impoverished mother sent him and his brother to an orphanage. There, while working odd jobs, he discovered that he was a natural athlete and started playing for local baseball teams. Eventually he landed a spot in the major leagues, where he played for eight years and was known for his baserunning.

While he was playing as an outfielder for the Chicago White Stockings in 1886 or 1887, he and a few of his teammates went out on the town for their day off. At one street corner, he heard a gospel preaching team from the Pacific Garden Mission singing the hymn "Where Is My Wandering Boy Tonight?"—which had been his mother's favorite hymn. He stopped to listen to the group and then began attending church services at the mission. There he was converted. Following his conversion, Sunday denounced drinking, swearing, and gambling and then began speaking in churches and at YMCAs.

As he developed his skills as a pulpit evangelist, he became the nation's most famous evangelist with his "colloquial sermons and frenetic delivery." Consider this example of his engaging speaking style: "I'm against sin. I'll kick it as long as I've got a foot, and I'll fight it as long as I've got a fist. I'll butt it as long as I've got a head. I'll bite it as long as I've got a tooth. And when I'm old and fistless and footless and toothless, I'll gum it 'til I go home to Glory and it goes home to perdition!"[12]

He held evangelistic campaigns in America's biggest cities, attracting the largest crowds of any evangelist before the advent of electronic sound systems.[13] He held some 300 crusades in thirty-nine years, and it was estimated that he addressed over 100 million people. More than a million people professed their faith in Christ under his preaching. One longtime associate called him "the greatest gospel preacher since the Apostle Paul."[14]

Of course, it was his association with Wilbur Chapman that propelled his work. Sunday's first crusade in 1896 was made up basically of Chapman's sermons. It was said of the pair that no two men were ever more different in their methods; no two ever agreed more completely on their message.[15]

In 1924, a group of businessmen invited Billy Sunday to hold an evangelistic campaign in Charlotte, North Carolina. The campaign was successful—in fact, ultimately far more successful than Sunday, riding high on Edward Kimble's original wave, could have realized at the time. During the revival meeting, a group of men formed a prayer group to pray for the world, specifically for Charlotte to have another great revival. This later resulted in the group inviting another evangelist, Mordecai Ham, to Charlotte to continue the campaign.

Born on a family farm in southern Kentucky, Mr. Ham descended from eight generations of Baptist preachers. "From the time I was eight years old," he once stated, "I never thought of myself as anything but a Christian. At nine, I had definite convictions that the Lord wanted me to preach."

However, in his youth and early twenties, he felt more drawn to making money in business. After attending college, he moved to Chicago, where he started as a salesman and then owned a business. He said, "My call to the ministry was a continuous and irresistible urge. I fought it when I started out as a salesman, because God had not completely whipped me, and I did not want to be a preacher until I had first made a fortune."[16] In December 1900, he finally capitulated to the calling he felt, closed his business, and devoted his life full-time to the ministry.

He experienced such tremendous success throughout the South that he was in great demand. He saw over 300,000 converts baptized between 1902 and 1940. Over 7,000 people surrendered to full-time Christian service under his preaching.

In 1934, after being asked by Billy Sunday's prayer group, Ham traveled to Charlotte, North Carolina, to run an evangelistic campaign. The crusade went well enough, though it did not have many converts. But on one of the last nights under the big tent, a tall, lanky young man walked up the aisle to receive Christ. That man would eventually take the ripple started by Edward Kimble and turned into a wave by D. L. Moody, Frederick Meyer, Wilbur Chapman, Billy Sunday, and Mordecai Ham and amplify it into a global tsunami of Christian ministry. That young man was Billy Graham.

WAVEMAKER WISDOM

The ripple effect of our choices and actions, however insignificant they may seem in the moment, carry on not only beyond what we can see but through time and generations. We should never underestimate our long-term impact, even though we tend to overestimate or grow frustrated by our immediate impact or apparent lack thereof.

What seeds are you planting today that will be harvested by future generations? As Chris Brady says, "Twenty years from now, what will you wish you had done today?

CHAPTER SIX

AN UNREASONABLE MAN*

The reasonable man adapts himself to the world; the unreasonable one persists in trying to adapt the world to himself. Therefore all progress depends on the unreasonable man.

—GEORGE BERNARD SHAW

The bell rang at the end of the last day of school in 1947, and Ralph, an eighth grader, barreled to the exit doors with his friends. As they passed a girl in their class, one of the boys' classmates blistered her by saying, "What a pig." As another of his classmates seconded the insult with a loud and vicious, "Ugh," Ralph looked back at the girl and saw her shattered expression.

Ralph was stunned; never before had he witnessed such cruelty, especially toward a friendly, helpful girl who had been in the same class with them since first grade and

* The title "An Unreasonable Man" is taken from the documentary film by the same name. See anunreasonableman.com.

whom everyone liked. He pondered the incident on his walk home and throughout the evening, unable to shake the image of that young girl's crestfallen expression and the sneer on the face of the classmate who had hurled the insult. He would never forget that incident, and his sensitivity to it and any form of injustice would prove to be the hallmark of his life.

Also apparent from an early age was his insatiable intellectual curiosity. In third grade, his teacher made a reference to the local "Beardsley Public Library." He frequently visited the library and knew otherwise. "Miss Franklin," he corrected her in front of the class, "the Beardsley and Memorial Library isn't a public library; it's a memorial library." His correction earned him a trip to the dunce chair in the corner.[1]

Ralph's inborn sensitivity and curiosity were cultivated, shaped, and amplified by his family life. At the age of ten, he arrived home from grade school, and his father asked him, "What did you learn today? Did you learn how to believe or did you learn how to think?"[2] That question perfectly exemplified the intellectual environment of their home.

His father, Nathra, a Lebanese immigrant, loved the Socratic method of asking open-ended questions, and family meals were usually spent debating the questions he posed, such as "So what about the leader theory of history? Do leaders make changes, or do they largely reflect dynamic pressures on the ground?" or "How did the Treaty of Versailles affect the economic conditions facing a devastated Germany after World War I?"[3]

Ralph's sister Laura wrote:

> My father's most passionate issue was justice—after all, Lebanon was colonized by the Ottomans, by the French; such colonization included the rest of the Arab world and included other European powers like the British. My father had made the USA his new home and country and was as passionate about justice through law here as elsewhere. I was not intimidated by my father—he helped his children to learn how to think critically.[4]

At heated dinner-table discussions, no one was allowed to become upset. Ralph's sister Claire recalled, "We were never allowed to run under fire....You had to stand your ground and talk it out."[5]

Ralph's parents were avid readers, and their love of reading was passed down to their children. Ralph later wrote:

> I liked books about the Wild West and the struggles between colonizers...and the Indians...History books, books on geography, on the great inventors (Whitney, Fulton, Bell, Edison) and explorers, ancient plays from Greece and Rome and modern classics by the legendary American muckrakers (Lincoln Steffens, Ida Tarbell, Upton Sinclair, George Seldes, and Ferdinand Lundberg). These books weren't assigned by our teachers."[6]

He and his siblings discussed and debated everything they read with their parents, challenging assumptions of the authors, analyzing ideas from different angles, and questioning everything.

Ralph's father had a voracious appetite for studying history. Never content with pat answers and always suspicious of hidden agendas, he believed that history was written and revised by people with vested interests. For instance, whenever he heard people say that Columbus discovered America, Nathra would laugh and ask, "Didn't the people who greeted him on the shore arrive before he did?"[7]

Ralph's brother, Shafeek, shared their father's interest in history. He studied American history in great depth and, like their father, was quick to point out anything that had been glossed over or distorted. Shafeek convinced their parents to purchase a brand-new set of the *Encyclopedia Americana*. One day he read a passage to Ralph from the article on Hawaii, which referred vaguely to "'external influence' that had caused tumult for 'the Kingdom of Hawaii' in the late nineteenth century." Shafeek looked up at Ralph after he finished reading the article and said, "Do you know what really happened? The Dole family, other Anglo planters, and some missionaries engineered a coup to overthrow the indigenous Hawaiian monarchy. This was no 'request of the people.' It was simple colonial imperialism, secured by the U.S. Marines. The encyclopedia is whitewashing history."[8]

Ralph's parents were also model citizens. They taught Ralph and his siblings to actively participate in their communities, to pay attention to local issues, to speak out and work to change things they didn't like. Ralph's parents frequently attended and spoke up at town meetings. They visited with local officials and newspaper editors to promote their opinions. They urged their friends and neighbors to be informed about issues and to vote. Ralph wrote that "they intuited what Marcus Cicero said over two thousand years ago in ancient Rome: 'Freedom is participation in power.'"[9] His sister Laura said "Success was not a word I heard at home. Purpose was central, as was the need to do a good job at whatever we did and to contribute to the larger society."[10]

Ralph's father owned a restaurant, which became a community hub. Nathra was a constant critic of power and was not shy about voicing his opinions. One time after he had spoken his mind, a customer cautioned, "How do you expect to make a profit if you keep speaking out that way?" Nathra responded, "When I sailed past the Statue of Liberty, I took it seriously."[11]

Occasionally, Nathra's nonconformist opinions prompted restaurant customers to question his patriotism. "Love it or leave it," they would taunt him.

But Nathra would not be deterred and loved turning the tables on them. "Do you love your country?" he would ask.

"You're damn right I do."

"Well, why don't you spend time improving it?" he would reply.

Ralph's mother, Rose, who had also immigrated from Lebanon, would ask Ralph similar questions. "Ralph, do you love your country?" she once asked him when he was about eight.

"Yes, Mother."

"Well, I hope when you grow up, you'll work hard to make it more lovable."[12]

Ralph was also taught to be a leader. "Turn your back on the pack," his mother would often tell him.

At eight years old, Ralph complained about having to wear short pants to school every day when all the other boys wore long pants. "Mother," he whined, "their mothers let them wear long pants."

His mother replied, "Well, they have their mothers and you have yours. Besides, why are you worried about being a little different?"[13]

Hard work was another trait instilled into Ralph and his siblings by their parents. Ralph's first job as a boy was a paper route, and he worked all through his youth. Nathra expressed their view on work to Ralph's sister Claire one day as they were walking home and passed a street cleaner. "I'm glad I'll never have to do such dirty work," Claire said.

Nathra stopped and said soberly, "Then you should always respect street cleaners, if only because they're doing work that you don't want to do, but that you very much want to have done. This is the same reason they should be paid well. Claire, as you grow up, you'll see all kinds of work being done. Don't look down on people for the work they do—and don't be in awe of anyone, either."[14]

Because of his parents' legacy, Ralph Nader has become a noble champion to some, an aggravating pest to others, and regardless of how you may feel about him, a Wavemaker for all. He was listed by the *Atlantic* among the 100 most influential figures in American history, one of only four living people to receive the honor.

Your legacy extends far beyond what you do personally. It extends to your children and what they make of their lives.

How are you instilling your most cherished values into your children? Have you created a safe environment for them to discuss and debate great ideas? Are you encouraging them to read, and do they see you reading often?

From the time that he was a young boy, spurred by sitting in courtrooms with his father, Ralph dreamed of becoming a lawyer, with the ultimate intention of promoting social justice. In high school, he was studious and something of a loner. As a freshman he brought home a stack of the *Congressional Record*, given to him by his principal, and pored over them to learn how Congress works.

He graduated with honors from high school and chose Princeton for his undergraduate studies. Although he qualified for an academic scholarship, his father, who had saved for years for his children's education, felt that scholarships should be applied to families who could not afford to pay tuition. Ralph was surprised to discover that few Princeton students shared his love for learning. Thus, he remained a loner and spent most of his free time reading in the library.

When Ralph was a junior, he noticed a trail of dead birds along his route to class. He realized that the same thing had happened at the same time of year for his previous two years in college, when DDT was sprayed to suppress the mosquito population. Worried that the chemical might also be harmful to students, he wrote several letters to the student newspaper. When his letters went unnoticed, he took a dead bird to the editor. "If it was harmful, they wouldn't do it," the editor told him. Ralph wrote that the editor's attitude was "A perfect case of the insults men will tolerate if they're conditioned to trust the system."[15]

After graduating magna cum laude, Ralph entered Harvard Law School. He joined the staff of the *Harvard Law School Record* on October 27, 1955, and began writing critical articles on subjects such as capital punishment and the plight of Native Americans. Ralph was later elected president of the *Record* and immediately tried to transform it into an investigative journal. He was met with resistance by both the staff and the school, so he resigned from the position but continued to write muckraking articles as a senior editor.

Ralph found focus when he stumbled across an article by fellow Harvard writer Harold A. Katz entitled "Liability of Automobile Manufacturers for Unsafe Design of Passenger Cars," in which Katz wrote:

> Automobile manufacturers have been negligent in failing to design and market reasonably safe automobiles. This failure has created a vast area of unnecessary hazard to human life and is a substantial contributing cause of the high injury and fatality rate in motorcar accidents....Nothing in law or logic insulates manufacturers from liability for deficiencies to design any more than for defects in construction.[16]

Auto safety became Nader's main course of study for his final year of law school. His final paper, which received an *A*, was entitled "Automotive Design Safety and Legal Liability."

Ralph graduated from Harvard in 1958. Wanting to avoid the military draft, which meant a longer term of service in poor conditions, he joined the army, where he spent six months as a cook. He spent the next few years traveling, writing, and occasionally practicing law. In 1959, he published an article in *The Nation* magazine entitled "The Safe Car You Can't Buy," which blasted the shortcomings of American car design. "It is clear that Detroit today is designing automobiles for style, cost, performance, and calculated obsolescence," he wrote, "but not—despite the 5,000,000 reported accidents, nearly 40,000 fatalities, 110,000 permanent disabilities and 1,500,000 injuries yearly—for safety."[17]

In 1964, Nader received a call from Assistant Labor Secretary Daniel P. Moynihan, who had read Nader's article and believed auto safety was the country's biggest public health concern. Moynihan offered Nader a consulting job on his planning staff regarding the issue of auto safety. Nader accepted, hitchhiked to Washington DC with one suitcase, and immediately began writing a report.

Ralph kept erratic hours and often worked late into the night. In the spring of 1965, he completed his groundbreaking report, wherein he concluded that the president should create a federal highway transportation agency, which would later become a reality.

Soon after, publisher Richard Grossman asked Nader to write a book about auto safety. On November 30, 1965, 11,000 copies of Nader's book, *Unsafe at Any Speed: The Designed-In Dangers of the American Automobile*, were printed. The book focused primarily on GM's Corvair, which Nader claimed had an engineering flaw that was causing accidents. One hundred damage suits had been filed involving that model, although GM denied culpability and blamed drivers for accidents. The next year, as a result of Nader's book, sales of the Corvair were down by 42 percent.

In January 1966, Nader began suspecting that he was being tailed and investigated by GM. On several occasions he noticed men hovering near him. He began receiving intimidating crank calls. On January 14, 1966, Senator Abraham Ribicoff invited Nader to provide testimony on auto safety concerns before a Senate subcommittee. The next day, Nader returned to the Senate building for a television interview. Just before he entered the pressroom, two men showed up and told the security guard at the desk that they were detectives and asked where Nader had gone. Nader now had proof that he was under surveillance, and Senator Ribicoff promptly ordered an investigation, citing harassment of a congressional witness. The *Washington Post* published a story about it the following Sunday.

Still, the harassment continued. Nader contacted a reporter at the *New Republic* and divulged details of the harassment. On March 4, 1966, the article was published and ignited a media frenzy. Several of the big auto companies denied any involvement, but GM remained silent. Five days later, GM issued a press release stating that they had initiated an investigation to determine whether Nader was acting on behalf of people who had filed lawsuits over the Corvair.

Senator Ribicoff was furious and immediately called a hearing. In Nader's testimony, he adamantly denied involvement in any Corvair litigation and stated, "They simply cannot understand that the prevention of cruelty to humans can be a sufficient motivation for one endeavoring to obtain the manufacture of safer cars."[18] Following his testimony, Nader became a celebrity. *Unsafe at Any Speed* shot to the top of bestseller lists. On November 14,

1966, Nader filed a $26 million suit against GM for invasion of privacy.

Nader's fight with GM had created a market for the type of law he had always envisioned practicing: legal advocacy for the public, which he now terms "responsive law." He turned his attention to the meat-packing industry, which he claimed was not adequately inspecting meat due to loopholes in legislation. In the summer of 1967, he published two articles on the subject that gained attention. Due in large part to Nader's activism, on October 31, 1967, the House passed a bill that effectively closed the loopholes. Though the bill was much weaker than Nader would have liked, this victory branded him as an all-around consumer activist.

Nader was becoming increasingly skillful at leveraging the media to get attention. The January 22, 1968 cover of *Newsweek* showed an image of Ralph Nader in a suit of armor, positioning him as a "consumer crusader."

That year, Nader began focusing on various causes, including inhumane working conditions in coal mines, what he felt were flaws in the Freedom of Information Act, issues with wholesale poultry products, radiation from medical X-rays, nuclear energy, and unsafe natural gas pipelines. His efforts led to the creation of the Natural Gas Pipeline Safety Act of 1968, the Wholesome Poultry Products Act, and the Radiation Control for Health and Safety Act.

Nader was amassing public support and was ready to take on more issues. But he couldn't do it alone. When he received a letter from students of Harvard Law School interested in helping him with his causes, Ralph formed a team consisting of seven members, who were soon dubbed "Nader's Raiders."

Their first assignment from Nader was to investigate the Federal Trade Commission (FTC). The FTC's job was to regulate unfair and deceptive business practices, but Nader and his team felt that it was no longer fulfilling its purpose. Their report filed on January 6, 1969, provided detailed evidence of indolence and ineptitude within the agency. And it spurred an independent investigation by the American Bar Association, which also concluded that the agency was riddled by divided leadership, incompetence, misallocation of funds, and other failures. President Nixon replaced Chairman Paul Dixon with Caspar Weinberger, who implemented sweeping changes.

Nader's next crusade was revealed when three mine workers from the United Mine Workers of America (UMWA) asked to meet with him on May 3, 1969. The men charged the UMWA president, Tony Boyle, with bullying, corruption, and apathy toward the working conditions faced by miners. Nader urged one of the men, Jock Yablonski, to run against Boyle in the next union election. "If I do run, Ralph," Yablonski said, "they'll try to kill me." Nader replied, "They wouldn't dare—you'll be in a goldfish bowl."[19]

Eventually, Yablonski did decide to run, with the objectives of purifying the union, returning to a more democratic process, and protecting the health and safety of union members. But when Boyle's men tampered with the votes, Yablonski lost the election. Knowing the election had been tainted, Yablonski promptly demanded an investigation. In January 1970, Yablonski was murdered, along with his wife and daughter, by contract killers ordered by Boyle. The killers were caught and sentenced, and Boyle was later convicted of conspiracy to commit murder and given a life sentence. Though the triple murder was tragic, the efforts of Nader and Yablonski led to the passage of the Coal Mine Health and Safety Act of 1969.

On the heels of his successes, Nader expanded his operation. Through several foundation grants and money earned from the sales of *Unsafe at Any Speed*, he founded the Center for the Study of Responsive Law and leased a building in Washington DC for the operation. In the summer of 1969, the center received 30,000 applications from people eager to join the cause, although they were only paid between $150 and $300 per week. Nader hired 200 of them.

The Raiders were given complete freedom to attack targets set by Nader, such as failures by the Food and Drug Administration, mine safety, air pollution, and the Department of Agriculture. They worked long, hard hours and were given no vacations. Sheila Harty, a former Raider, expressed how they all felt: "As a Nader Raider, I was an avenging angel against modern sins, like environmental pollution, occupational disease and injury, deceptive advertising, and corporate accountability. In fact, I've never since been so content with employment. I often wondered why I felt so at home."[20]

Most people are far more motivated by a worthy cause than by money. People want to feel as if they're part of something bigger than themselves. They want to feel that they're truly making a difference.

Are you merely dangling carrots in front of your people, or are you enlisting them in a great cause? How effectively are you articulating your vision? Further, are you expending your energies toward something that matters to you (and others)?

No government agency or big business was immune from the Raiders' relentless attacks. Nader read six newspapers a day in a vigilant search for injustice. But when the team filed reports criticizing the Interstate Commerce Commission, the Food and Drug Administration, and the National Air Pollution Control Administration, they began falling out of favor with influential politicians, who felt that the attacks were personal and unjustified. And when a bill to create a consumer protection agency was watered down far beyond Nader's original vision, he became disillusioned with Congress.

He began focusing his efforts on grassroots, local politics. After he gave a speech to Miss Porter's School, a private boarding school for girls in Farmington, Connecticut, some girls from the audience approached him and asked him how they could join the fight. Nader formed a new team of investigative workers and targeted nursing homes. Several girls spent an entire summer in Washington DC, dubbing themselves the "Maiden Muckrakers." Nader said, "They worked in nursing homes, they came to Washington, they researched, they wrote a book, and then they went on radio and TV, testified before Congress. And all this concern led to one of our associates starting the National Coalition for Nursing Home Reform, and she's still at it, with chapters all over the country."[21]

In 1970, Nader helped a pair of Harvard law graduates execute a plan to hold GM accountable for safety and pollution issues. The campaign was successful and groundbreaking, and GM was forced to higher standards of accountability and transparency to consumers and shareholders. Later that year, Nader settled his privacy suit against GM and received $425,000, which was the highest amount ever collected in a case of that nature at the time. Nader invested the money in a new legal firm, the Public Interest Research Group, and hired thirteen young attorneys to run the office. It wasn't long before the firm was flooded with new cases.

After six more years of crusading, in 1976, the first hints at a Nader presidential campaign emerged in the press. But Nader was not interested in becoming a politician. Rather, he saw himself as an outside influencer. After a meeting with Jimmy Carter, Ralph threw his support behind the presidential hopeful. Carter won the election by a narrow margin. To Nader's disappointment, Carter was too much of a people pleaser to keep most of the promises he had made to Nader, and Nader soon withdrew his support.

Around this time, Nader experienced a fairly sudden decline in popularity, after two journalists published two books criticizing his goals and tactics. One of them, *Hit and Run: The Rise—and Fall?—of Ralph Nader* by Ralph de Toledano, said on the dust jacket:

> Nader's consumerism has little to do with the consumer, with improved products and services, or with the needs of the citizenry. It is an ideologically motivated effort to take control of industry from the producers and to turn it over to government and to the Naderites. This is statism, pure and simple—a kind of national socialism since Nader suffers from a suspicion of foreign countries bordering on xenophobia. It is this which converted and debased the legitimate concerns of the true consumers into a politically destructive force, which sowed distrust and suspicion of all the institutions of this country.[22]

There was truth to de Toledano's perspective, and Nader's efforts were further impeded when Ronald Reagan, a big business–supporting Republican, took the White House in 1980. In a letter to Reagan in 1982, Nader accused him of siding with corporations to the detriment of citizens and complained that the federal government was eroding consumer protection. When Reagan's administration was less than responsive, Nader realized that his efforts would be largely wasted dealing with the government and once again turned his attention back to the people. He wrote, "Banding together as buyers can broaden and metabolize the community quest for economic justice and liberate both political and economic thinkers from their invisible chains of thought."[23]

WAVEMAKER WISDOM

When doors slam in your face, find open windows to go through. Never confuse your objective with your tactics; an infinite number of tactics can be used to achieve the same objective.

Where have you been shut down in your efforts to achieve an objective? How can you get creative in finding new avenues for progress?

In 1982, Nader founded the organization Essential Information to encourage citizenship and to promote issues not covered by the mainstream press. Three years later, he helped create the Foundation for Taxpayer and Consumer Rights. He was masterful at setting up organizations and then, once they were off the ground, stepping away and letting them run on their own, independent of his direct involvement. He spent the majority of his time traveling and speaking across the country.

In 1986, he published another book, *The Big Boys*, an examination of corporate power and the men who wield it. Despite that coup, the year was personally devastating to Nader. He developed Bell's palsy, which causes facial muscles to become weak or paralyzed. But that was a minor issue compared to the death of his brother, Shafeek, with whom Nader had been very close all his life. Ralph went into seclusion to grieve and regroup.

In truth, he had much to ponder. Those in power saw him as a pesky irritator and agitator. People in his trenches were tired of fighting long, hard battles that resulted at best in weak legislation. There were costs to Nader's victories, as consumers paid higher prices for new cars with safety features, such as seat belts, padded dashboards, and air bags. Paychecks were eroded by mandatory deductions to support the Occupational Health and Safety Administration (OSHA).

But Ralph was not close to giving up. In 1989, he went back to Princeton and recommended that the graduating class should be more involved and effective at combating social ills. His ideas developed into a nonprofit organization, Princeton Project 55. He created a new advocacy group, the Taxpayer Assets Project, with the purpose of finding and addressing areas where taxpayer assets were mismanaged. Of particular interest was the issue of the federal government awarding intellectual property to corporations from research funded by tax dollars. He was involved in several more projects in 1989 and told a friend that "Things are popping again."[24]

On July 7, 1991, Nader suffered another profound loss when his father died at the age of ninety-nine. Ralph grieved again. He was further disappointed as many of his previous efforts were being dismantled. As his friend Marcus Raskin put it, "What he saw happening was that everything he stood for was being taken away piece by piece."[25]

Yet, carrying the banner of his father's legacy, he reentered the fray, this time in a role that he'd never considered before. He entered the 1992 presidential election, though in typical Nader fashion. Believing that neither political party truly served the people, he remained independent. "I'm 'none of the above,' and I'm not running for president," he said. "I'm running for a citizen's empowerment agenda."[26] He urged citizens to write him in on the ballot as a protest and began stumping in New Hampshire to impact the primary election in the state. Without even trying, he raised $80,000 and had about 1,000 volunteers join his campaign.

His agenda was to urge people to become responsible citizens and not sit silently on the sidelines as powerful vested interests eroded their rights. His campaign was moderately influential, though Bill Clinton won the election.

Initially, Nader was guardedly pleased with the result, but he soon took issue with many of Clinton's policies. "In [Clinton's] first three years of his tenure," Ralph wrote, "he's been consistently on the side of big business when it's conflicted with labor and consumers."[27]

When the 1996 election arrived, Nader referred to Clinton and his Republican rival, Bob Dole, as "Tweedledee and Tweedledum." But needing the backing of an official party to get on the ballot in most states, he threw his hat into the ring as a Green Party candidate, though he was not a member of the party. As is typical with third-party candidates in the United States, Nader was dubbed an election "spoiler." He responded, "These parties are not offering an adequate choice given their duopoly over politics. Clinton has become George Ronald Clinton...giving in to one corporate demand after another, not fighting back and drawing the line against Dole and Gingrich on the deregulation of health and safety agencies."[28]

In accepting the Green Party nomination, he revealed an insight into his motivations and character. When he took the podium to accept the nomination, the crowd chanted, "Go, Ralph, go! Go, Ralph, go!" He asked the crowd for silence and said, "The intonation should be, 'Go, *we* go!'" Though Nader secured spots on the ballots in just twenty-two states and earned only 1 percent of the popular vote, the campaign gave a voice to his causes.

Furthermore, it set the stage for his most serious—and most famous (or infamous, depending on one's views)—presidential campaign in 2000. This time, the Republican contenders were Texas Governor George W. Bush and Senator John McCain of Arizona, and the Democratic candidates were former Senator Bill Bradley from New Jersey and incumbent Vice President Al Gore. Pat Buchanan joined Nader as an independent with the Reform Party.

Nader started the campaign by raising awareness for the Commission on Presidential Debates (CPD), a private corporation that regulates how presidential debates are conducted. The CPD requires that any candidate wishing to debate must meet the following criteria:

1. Evidence of Constitutional Eligibility: The candidate must be at least thirty-five years of age and be a natural born citizen of the United States.
2. Evidence of Ballot Access: A candidate must appear on enough state ballots to have a mathematical chance of winning enough electoral votes (270) to secure the presidency.
3. Indicators of Electoral Support: As determined by an average of five national polling organizations, a candidate must have at least a 15 percent approval ratio from the national electorate.

The third criterion is a paradox, Nader argued, because the polling companies are owned by at least three major media corporations. And because none cover third-party campaigns, there would be little chance of gaining the required poll ratings.

Still, he declared his candidacy on February 21, 2000, with the campaign slogan, "Nader 2000: Government of, by, and for the people...not monitored interests." The most important focus of his campaign was revealed in a speech to the L.A. Press Club:

> The central contention of politics should be
> the distribution of power. That is where a political

campaign should be first and foremost. The most important question that a candidate can ask the people during the campaign is, "Do you want to be more powerful as a voter, citizen, consumer, worker, taxpayer, and small saver–investor? Or do you want to continue to be rolled and dominated and manip-ulated by the concentration of power and wealth in too few hands who then establish the supremacy of the political economy over the majority of the people in this country?"[29]

Despite his best efforts, Nader was barred from all pres-idential debates. In two cases, he was forcefully prevented by police officers from even entering the buildings in which debates were taking place. Though he filed a lawsuit against the CPD in federal district court, the debates were over.

But Nader pressed on, not knowing the drama that would unfold in weeks to come. A ripple that had begun at the dinner table with his family was building to a wave that he could never have predicted, let alone controlled.

Republicans welcomed his presence in the race, knowing he wasn't draining votes from their candidate. But Democrats and many in the press begged him to drop out of the race, branding him a spoiler. The denigrating label was hurled with even greater vitriol when the elec-tion hinged on a race too close to call in Florida. A hand recount was commissioned, and the election eventually fell to Bush. Outraged Democrats accused Nader of handing the election to Bush by taking away votes that would have gone to Gore.

Though Nader responded, "You can't spoil a system that is spoiled to the core,"[30] he undoubtedly would have preferred Gore to Bush. But he was left to deal with the unintended consequences of his actions.

WAVEMAKER WISDOM

It's been said that "Whoever lifts one end of the stick also lifts the other." Likewise, Wavemakers can start the splash, but they can't control where the ripples go. There will always be unintended consequences that follow from your direct actions.

Two things to learn from this: (1) when you take a bold stand for anything, you must be prepared to deal with consequences that you may not have intended and that you may not like, and (2) you must be certain that you are doing the right thing. With that certainty, you can "let the chips fall where they may," as the saying goes. But you might look back on your actions and realize that you made a mistake.

Are you prepared to deal with unintended consequences? Are you absolutely certain that you are on the right track, that you are doing the right things for the right reasons?

Since the 2000 election, Nader has not backed down or diminished his efforts. He was heavily involved in the antitrust case against Microsoft. He was a vocal critic during the Enron scandal. He declared the Patriot Act unconstitutional. He has run for president two more times, in 2004 and 2008, in order to raise awareness for his causes. To this day, he champions a wide variety of social justice causes.

Whether or not you agree with Ralph's views and tactics, he remains a powerful example of the principle that one person can make a profound difference. As he told students in a high school commencement address in 1970, "Almost every significant breakthrough has come from the spark, the drive, the initiative of one person. You must believe this." Of course, he had learned this from his father who taught him: "The greatest obstacle to good government in a democracy is the feeling by too many citizens that they just don't count."[31]

Individual citizens *can* count, they *can* matter, and they *can* turn their small ripples of influence into monumental waves. And Ralph Nader, an "unreasonable" and tireless crusader for social justice, is a powerful example of how this can be done.

CHAPTER SEVEN

A BLOW TO BIG BROTHER

They who would give up essential Liberty, to purchase a little temporary Safety, deserve neither Liberty nor Safety.

—ATTRIBUTED TO BENJAMIN FRANKLIN

On November 20, 1787, an article appeared in *The Independent Journal*, a periodical serving the American colony of New York. The article, entitled "Consequences of Hostilities Between the States," was published anonymously under the pseudonym "Publius." The author wrote:

> Safety from external danger is the most powerful director of national conduct. Even the ardent love of liberty will, after a time, give way to its dictates. The violent destruction of life and property incident to war, the continual effort and alarm attendant on a state of continual danger, will compel nations the most attached to liberty to resort for repose and

security to institutions which have a tendency to destroy their civil and political rights. **To be more safe, they at length become willing to run the risk of being less free**.

The institutions chiefly alluded to are standing armies and the **correspondent appendages of military establishments** [emphasis added].

Later, it was revealed that the author was Alexander Hamilton, and the article is now known as *Federalist* paper #8.

In 1949, the world was introduced to Winston Smith, a middle-class civil servant who wrote in his journal, while hiding from cameras in the alcove of his one-bedroom apartment, "Thoughtcrime does not entail death. Thoughtcrime IS death." Winston is the protagonist of George Orwell's famous novel *1984* who writhes under the clutches of Big Brother, the dictator of the totalitarian state Oceania. Big Brother rules by ubiquitous surveillance of all citizens and propaganda with the theme, "Big Brother is watching you."

On January 17, 1961, US President Dwight D. Eisenhower gave his farewell address to the nation, wherein he warned:

A vital element in keeping the peace is our military establishment. Our arms must be mighty, ready for instant action, so that no potential aggressor may be tempted to risk his own destruction.

Our military organization today bears little relation to that known by any of my predecessors in peacetime, or indeed by the fighting men of World War II or Korea.

Until the latest of our world conflicts, the United States had no armaments industry. American makers of plowshares could, with time and as required, make swords as well. But now we can no longer risk emergency improvisation of national defense; we have been compelled to create a permanent armaments industry of vast proportions. Added to this, three and a half million men and women are directly engaged in the defense establishment. We annually spend on military security more than the net income of all United States corporations.

This conjunction of an immense military establishment and a large arms industry is new in the American experience. The total influence—economic, political, even spiritual—is felt in every city, every State house, every office of the Federal government. We recognize the imperative need for this development. Yet we must not fail to comprehend its grave implications. Our toil, resources and livelihood are all involved; so is the very structure of our society.

In the councils of government, we must guard against the acquisition of unwarranted influence, whether sought or unsought, by the military industrial complex. The potential for the disastrous rise of misplaced power exists and will persist.

We must never let the weight of this combination endanger our liberties or democratic processes.

We should take nothing for granted. *Only an alert and knowledgeable citizenry* **can compel the proper meshing of the huge industrial and military machinery of defense with our peaceful methods and goals, so that security and liberty may prosper together** [emphasis added].

On June 5, 2013, the world was shocked by allegations from an "alert and knowledgeable citizen" who warned that Big Brother was alive and well, that "unwarranted influence" was being wielded by "appendages of military establishments." In an interview with a reporter this citizen revealed:

> [The National Security Agency (NSA)] and intelligence community in general is focused on getting intelligence wherever it can by any means possible. It believes, on the grounds of sort of a self-certification, that they serve the national interest. Originally we saw that focus very narrowly tailored as foreign intelligence gathered overseas.
>
> Now increasingly we see that it's happening domestically and to do that they, the NSA specifically, targets the communications of everyone. It ingests them by default. It collects them in its system and it filters them and it analyses them and it measures them and it stores them for periods of time simply because that's the easiest, most efficient, and most valuable way to achieve these ends. So while they may be intending to target someone associated with

a foreign government or someone they suspect of terrorism, they're collecting your communications to do so.

Any analyst at any time can target anyone, any selector, anywhere. Where those communications will be picked up depends on the range of the sensor networks and the authorities that analyst is empowered with. Not all analysts have the ability to target everything. But I sitting at my desk certainly had the authorities to wiretap anyone from you or your accountant to a Federal judge to even the President if I had a personal e-mail.

That citizen is Edward Snowden, American computer specialist, former Central Intelligence Agency (CIA) employee, and former National Security Agency (NSA) contractor who disclosed classified NSA documents, which exposed a global surveillance system administered by the NSA. Depending on one's views, he's been labeled a traitor, hero, whistleblower, dissident, and patriot. And regardless of your perspective, he is most certainly a Wavemaker whose ripples are only beginning to be felt.

Little is known about Snowden, other than what his actions have revealed. As a child and in his youth, he was described by friends and neighbors as shy, quiet, and nice. One longtime friend said he has always been articulate. His father described him as "a sensitive, caring young man" and a "deep thinker."[1] Politically, Snowden is an independent. He has stated that he voted for a third-party candidate in the 2008 election, and political donation records show that he contributed to maverick Ron Paul in the 2012 election. By all accounts, he is brilliant.

He was born in 1983 and grew up in Wilmington, North Carolina. His father was an officer in the US Coast Guard, his mother a clerk at the United States District Court.

In 1999, the Snowdens moved to Ellicott City, Maryland. There, Edward studied at a community college to get the credits he needed for a high school diploma, but he did not complete the coursework owing to illness. He later passed the test to acquire his GED. "I don't think he even studied," one friend later reported. "He just showed up and passed." Snowden took community college courses on and off but never finished a degree. At the age of twenty, he wrote online that "Great minds do not need a university to make them any more credible: they get what they need and quietly blaze their trails into history."[2]

During high school, he developed a fascination for computer technology. One friend said that Edward "was a geek like the rest of us. We played video games, watched anime. It was before geek was cool."[3] He and his friends built computers from parts ordered over the Internet.

In 2001, Edward's parents divorced. His father moved to Pennsylvania and he stayed with his mother.

On May 7, 2004, Snowden enlisted in the United States Army Reserve as a Special Forces recruit, saying that he felt he "had an obligation as a human being to help free people from oppression."[4] But when he broke both legs in a training accident, he was discharged before completing the training.

He then took a job as an NSA security guard before joining the Central Intelligence Agency (CIA) to work on IT security in 2006. He had no trouble getting the CIA job because, as he put it, he was a "computer wizard." In 2007, he was stationed in Geneva, Switzerland, where he was given high security clearances and was responsible for maintaining computer network security. He later said that during his stay there, he witnessed an incident that proved to be "formative." The CIA deliberately got a Swiss banker drunk and then encouraged him to drive home, Snowden said. When the banker was later arrested, the CIA operative intervened and recruited him.

Mavanee Anderson, who worked with Edward in Geneva, said he spoke of the "stresses and burdens" of his work there and described Edward as "thoughtful and at times brooding." She reported that during that period, from 2007 to early 2009, he "was already experiencing a crisis of conscience of sorts." She later wrote, "I think anyone smart enough to be involved in the type of work he does, who is privy to the type of information to which he was privy, will have at least moments like these."[5]

Edward later said of his time there, "Much of what I saw in Geneva really disillusioned me about how my government functions and what its impact is in the world. I realized that I was part of something that was doing far more harm than good." He first started thinking about exposing government secrets in 2007 but chose not to because, as he said, "Most of the secrets the CIA has are about people, not machines and systems, so I didn't feel comfortable with disclosures that I thought could endanger anyone." He also said that Barack Obama's 2008 campaign promises gave him hope that there would be real reforms that would make public disclosure unnecessary.[6]

In 2009, Edward left the CIA to take a job as a private contractor with the computer company Dell, working inside an NSA facility on a US military base in Japan. He worked there for the next three years, earning an annual salary that he claimed was "roughly $200,000." There, he said, he "watched as Obama advanced the very policies that [he] thought would be reined in." He learned how broad and deep the NSA's reach was, claiming "they are intent on making every conversation and every form of behaviour in the world known to them." As a result, he said, "I got hardened." He said he learned from this experience that "you can't wait around for someone else to act. I had been looking for leaders, but I realized that leadership is about being the first to act."[7]

Snowden was reported to have begun downloading sensitive NSA material as early as April 2012. He took a significant pay cut to accept a job in Hawaii as an infrastructure analyst with consulting firm Booz Allen Hamilton because, as he said, the position "granted me access to lists of machines all over the world the NSA hacked." When asked by a reporter if he specifically went to Booz Allen Hamilton to gather evidence of surveillance, he replied, "Correct on Booz."[8]

It was reported that Snowden gained access to privileged information by persuading coworkers to give him their logins and passwords, but this was later refuted by NSA sources and Snowden himself. An NSA staffer went on record to say that Snowden was "given full administrator privileges, with virtually unlimited access to NSA data" because he could "do things nobody else could." "That kid was a genius among geniuses," the staffer said. "NSA is full of smart people, but anybody who sat in a meeting with Ed will tell you he was in a class of his own....I've never seen anything like it." Snowden was described as a "principled and ultra-competent, if somewhat eccentric employee, and one who earned the access used to pull off his leak by impressing superiors with sheer talent."[9]

During his stay in Hawaii, Snowden tried to express his concerns to employees and supervisors using "internal channels of dissent." But he was met with indifference. He said later in an interview:

> When you're in positions of privileged access like a systems administrator for these sort of intelligence community agencies, you're exposed to a lot more information on a broader scale than the average employee. And because of that you see things that may be disturbing. But over the course of a normal person's career you'd only see one or two of these instances. When you see everything you see them on a more frequent basis and you recognize that some of these things are actually abuses. And when you talk to people about them in a place like this where this is the normal state of business, people tend not to take them very seriously and move on from them.

But over time that awareness of wrongdoing sort of builds up and you feel compelled to talk about it. And the more you talk about it, the more you're ignored, the more you're told it's not a problem, until eventually you realize that these things need to be determined by the public and not by somebody who was simply hired by the government.[10]

WAVEMAKER WISDOM

Never be satisfied as a drone worker, just showing up and going through the conveyor-belt routines you're taught. In any position, always be looking for things to improve. And never, ever compromise your moral standards in the name of "Everyone is doing it."

Are you uncomfortable with anything you see at your workplace or in any other position in which you serve? What should you do about it? Why do you think so many people just go along with wrongs they see happening every day?

He decided to take matters into his own hands. In late 2012, he contacted Glenn Greenwald, a journalist at *The Guardian* newspaper in London. He remained anonymous and stated he had "sensitive documents" he would like to share. He also contacted documentary filmmaker Laura Poitras in January 2013, after seeing her documentary about NSA whistleblower William Binney. In April 2013, Snowden began providing documents to both of them. He told another reporter, Barton Gellman of *The Washington Post*, "I understand that I will be made to suffer for my actions, and that the return of this information to the public marks my end."[11]

In May 2013, Snowden asked for a temporary leave of absence, saying he needed treatment for his epilepsy. On May 20, he flew to Hong Kong and began disclosing documents to reporters. "All I can say right now," he said, "is the U.S. government is not going to be able to cover this up by jailing or murdering me. Truth is coming, and it cannot be stopped."[12] He also said, "My sole motive is to inform the public as to that which is done in their name and that which is done against them."[13] On July 12, he met with representatives of human rights organizations and declared:

> The 4th and 5th Amendments to the Constitution of my country, Article 12 of the Universal Declaration of Human Rights, and numerous statutes and treaties forbid such systems of massive, pervasive surveillance. While the U.S. Constitution marks these programs as illegal, my government argues that secret court rulings, which the world is not permitted to see, somehow legitimize an illegal affair....
>
> I believe in the principle declared at Nuremberg in 1945: "Individuals have international duties which transcend the national obligations of obedience. Therefore individual citizens have the duty to violate domestic laws to prevent crimes against peace and humanity from occurring."

WAVEMAKER WISDOM

When challenging the status quo on any front, it's critical that you do your homework and really understand what you're doing, what the opposition will try to do to you, and the full implications of your actions. In other words, education must precede activism, as Stephen Palmer put it in his book *Uncommon Sense: A Common Citizen's Guide to Rebuilding America*. Stephen writes, "Plainly put, we don't have enough widespread education to sustain an anger-driven revolution....It's not enough to just be mad; we must also be wise."

What battle are you fighting? Do you understand the moral, cultural, and legal ramifications in depth? As Stephen Palmer asks, "Is the depth of your education equal to the fervor of your opinions?"

Within months, Snowden's leaked documents had been published by media outlets across the globe, including *The New York Times*, *The Washington Post*, *The Guardian* (Britain), *Der Spiegel* (Germany), *O Globo* (Brazil), *Le Monde* (France), and other outlets in Sweden, Canada, Italy, Netherlands, Norway, Spain, and Australia. By November 2013, *The Guardian* had published one percent of the documents, with "the worst yet to come."

When asked how he could justify exposing intelligence methods that might benefit adversaries of the United States, he replied, "Perhaps I am naïve, but I believe that at this point in history, the greatest danger to our freedom and way of life comes from the reasonable fear of omniscient State powers kept in check by nothing more than policy documents." The steady expansion of surveillance powers, he wrote, is "such a direct threat to democratic governance that I have risked my life and family for it."[14]

When asked if he truly understood the risks of his disclosures, he replied:

> You can't come forward against the world's most powerful intelligence agencies and be completely free from risk because they're such powerful adversaries. No one can meaningfully oppose them. If they want to get you, they'll get you in time. But at the same time you have to make a determination about what it is that's important to you. And if living unfreely but comfortably is something you're willing to accept—and I think many of us are because it's human nature—you can get up every day, go to work, you can collect your large paycheck for relatively little work against the public interest, and go to sleep at night after watching your shows.
>
> But if you realize that that's the world you helped create and it's gonna get worse with the next generation and the next generation who extend the capabilities of this sort of architecture of oppression, you realize that you might be willing to accept any risk and it doesn't matter what the outcome is so long as the public gets to make their own decisions about how that's applied.[15]

And why should the public even care about surveillance? Snowden's answer:

> Because even if you're not doing anything wrong you're being watched and recorded. And the storage capability of these systems increases every year consistently by orders of magnitude to where it's getting to the point where you don't have to have done anything wrong. You simply have to eventually fall under suspicion from somebody even by a wrong call. And then they can use this system to go back in time and scrutinize every decision you've ever made, every friend you've ever discussed something with. And attack you on that basis to sort of derive suspicion from an innocent life and paint anyone in the context of a wrongdoer.

It didn't take long for the US government to paint Snowden as a wrongdoer. On June 14, 2013, shortly after his disclosures, federal prosecutors filed a criminal complaint against him and asked Hong Kong to detain him on a provisional arrest warrant. He was charged with theft of government property, "unauthorized communication of national defense information," and "willful communication of classified communications intelligence information to an unauthorized person."[16]

On June 22, while Snowden was en route to Ecuador, where he was seeking asylum, US officials revoked his passport. He landed at Moscow's Sheremetyevo International Airport for a layover on the 23rd, where he was stuck in the transit section of the airport for a month until the Russian government granted him a one-year temporary asylum on August 1. At the time of this writing, he remains in Russia at an undisclosed location while seeking permanent asylum in another country.

In early September 2013, Snowden dropped another bombshell when he revealed documents showing that the NSA was spying on government officials in other countries, including Brazil, France, Mexico, Britain, China, Germany, and Spain, as well as thirty-five world leaders. Mexico's foreign ministry swiftly issued a statement stating "Without prejudging the veracity of the information presented in the media, the Mexican government rejects and categorically condemns any espionage work against Mexican citizens in violation of international law." Brazil's foreign minister followed suit, calling the situation "an inadmissible and unacceptable violation of Brazilian sovereignty."[17] Tensions mounted between the Unites States and its allies who learned of the spying activities.

In December, Snowden wrote an open letter to the people of Brazil, wherein he stated, "There is a huge difference between legal programs, legitimate spying... and these programs of dragnet mass surveillance that put entire populations under an all-seeing eye and save copies forever....These programs were never about terrorism: they're about economic spying, social control, and diplomatic manipulation. They're about power."[18]

The world was given further insight into just how deep the rabbit hole goes when Snowden next revealed that the

US intelligence community was given a top secret "black budget," consisting of $52 billion for 2013, which allowed agencies to pay private tech companies in the States, including Apple, Facebook, Google, and Verizon, for "clandestine access" to their communications networks. Documentation showed:

> Under the Obama administration the communication records of millions of US citizens are being collected indiscriminately and in bulk—regardless of whether they are suspected of any wrongdoing. The secret Foreign Intelligence Surveillance Court [FISC or the FISA Court] granted the order to the FBI on April 25, giving the government unlimited authority to obtain the data.[19]

Further documentation revealed in November exposed the NSA's explicitly stated goal to "dramatically increase mastery of the global network" and "acquire the capabilities to gather intelligence on anyone, anytime, anywhere."[20]

Whether you love him or loathe him, agree or disagree with his actions, you must at least respect the purity of Snowden's intentions. In a note accompanying the first documents he disclosed, he wrote, "I understand that I will be made to suffer for my actions," but "I will be satisfied if the federation of secret law, unequal pardon and irresistible executive powers that rule the world that I love are revealed even for an instant." He has consistently and repeatedly insisted that he wants to avoid the spotlight, saying, "I don't want public attention because I don't want the story to be about me. I want it to be about what the U.S. government is doing."[21] Accordingly, he has turned down potentially millions of dollars in book and movie deals.[22]

The question remains whether or not Snowden has been effective at raising public awareness and catalyzing policy and legal changes to US surveillance efforts. As he has said, echoing the warning of Orwell's *1984*:

> The greatest fear that I have regarding the outcome for America of these disclosures is that nothing will change. People will see in the media all of these disclosures. They'll know the lengths that the government is going to grant themselves powers unilaterally to create greater control over American society and global society. But they won't be willing to take the risks necessary to stand up and fight to change things to force their representatives to actually take a stand in their interests.
>
> And the months ahead, the years ahead, it's only going to get worse until eventually there will be a time where policies will change because the only thing that restricts the activities of the surveillance state [is] policy. Even our agreements with other sovereign governments, we consider that to be a stipulation of policy rather than a stipulation of law. And because of that a new leader will be elected, they'll find the switch, say that "Because of the crisis, because of the dangers we face in the world, some new and unpredicted threat, we need more authority, we need more power." And there will be nothing the

people can do at that point to oppose it. And it will be turnkey tyranny.[23]

On December 23, 2013, Snowden declared that he had achieved his objective, telling *Washington Post* reporter Barton Gellman:

> For me, in terms of personal satisfaction, the mission's already accomplished. I already won. As soon as the journalists were able to work, everything that I had been trying to do was validated. Because, remember, I didn't want to change society. I wanted to give society a chance to determine if it should change itself. All I wanted was for the public to be able to have a say in how they are governed. That is a milestone we left a long time ago. Right now, all we are looking at are stretch goals.[24]

In early January 2014, Debbie Hines, a trial attorney writing for *The Huffington Post*, wrote:

> All of the focus on Edward Snowden and clemency, pardon, whistle blower status or jail misses the real point. Namely, the NSA is conducting what amounts to illegal surveillance on collections of telephone data of persons not to mention surveillance on everyone in the world, including everyday people, world leaders and perhaps even U.S. elected officials. Setting aside for the moment the issues surrounding Edward Snowden's legal dilemma, more focus needs to be placed on the issue of NSA

surveillance. Specifically, now that we have the information provided by Snowden, what are we going to do about it?[25]

Indeed, thanks to the efforts of Edward Snowden, the debate is sure to continue. He stood on the shoulders of Alexander Hamilton, George Orwell, Dwight D. Eisenhower, and many others to start a wave. It's now up to ordinary citizens to continue that wave long after Snowden is out of the spotlight. They must decide if they are willing to sacrifice "essential liberty" to "purchase a little temporary safety."

CHAPTER EIGHT

HOW TO BECOME A WAVEMAKER

As long as you don't make waves, ripples, life seems easy. But that's condemning yourself to impotence and death before you are dead.

—JEANNE MOREAU

An ancient Chinese parable is told of Yu Gong, a ninety-year-old man whose travels to and from his home were inconvenienced by two large nearby mountains. One day Yu Gong said to his family, "These mountains are in our way. Why not get rid of them?"

His son and grandson responded, "What you say is true. We shall start moving them tomorrow."

The next day, they began moving the mountain, carrying stones into the sea. They worked nonstop through summer and winter, rain and snow.

Observing their work, a man said, "Yu Gong, you are so old. Do you really think it is possible to move the mountains?"

Yu Gong responded, "When [my sons and I] die, my grandchildren will continue, and so on through generation after generation. We will move the stones every day and we will move these mountains."[1]

The parable expresses an Asian mindset, which has largely been lost in the western world. In his book *The Silent Language*, Edward Hall explains:

> The future to us is the foreseeable future, not the future of the Asian that may involve centuries....Anyone who has worked in industry or in the government of the United States has heard the following: "Gentlemen, this is for the long term! Five or ten years."...The Asian, however, feels that it is perfectly realistic to think of a long time in terms of thousands of years or even an endless period.[2]

The Iroquois Native American tribe shares a similar mindset, as manifested by their "Seventh Generation" tradition. "In every deliberation," they say, "we must consider the impact on the seventh generation...even if it requires having skin as thick as the bark of a pine." The tradition has its roots in the constitution of the Iroquois Nations, what they call "The Great Binding Law," which states:

> In all of your deliberations in the Confederate Council, in your efforts at law making, in all your official acts, self-interest shall be cast into oblivion. Cast not over your shoulder behind you the warnings of the nephews and nieces should they chide you for any error or wrong you may do, but return

to the way of the Great Law which is just and right. Look and listen for the welfare of the whole people and have always in view not only the present but also the coming generations, even those whose faces are yet beneath the surface of the ground—the unborn of the future Nation.[3]

Oren Lyons, chief of the Onondaga Nation, expounded by writing, "We are looking ahead, as is one of the first mandates given us as chiefs, to make sure and to make every decision that we make relate to the welfare and well-being of the seventh generation to come....What about the seventh generation? Where are you taking them? What will they have?"[4]

Generational thinking is the fundamental mindset of Wavemakers. Self-absorbed celebrities may make a big splash while they're alive, but their ripples die with them. It is only through self-sacrificing service and humble leadership that our ripples can become magnificent waves through generations. Wavemakers are such precisely because they think beyond satisfying their own needs and wants and pursuing their own pleasure. They apply their talents, energy, and resources to making the world a better place for posterity. This is the essence of Wavemaking.

> *A civilization flourishes when people plant trees under which they will never sit.*
> —Greek Proverb

The seven Wavemakers we've featured in this book— and indeed all Wavemakers in history—possessed a generational mindset, and this was a primary catalyst for their actions and a foundational component of their success.

In addition to cultivating generational thinking, there are specific ways you can follow their examples and become a Wavemaker yourself.

Five Factors That Determine the Size and Impact of Your Waves

Five factors influence the formation of waves and determine their size and magnitude in the ocean and other bodies of water:

1. Wind speed or strength relative to wave speed— the wind must be moving faster than the wave crest for energy transfer.
2. The uninterrupted distance of open water over which the wind blows without significant change in direction (called the "fetch").
3. Width of area affected by the fetch.
4. Wind duration—the time over which the wind has blown over a given area.
5. Water depth.[5]

The wave is the signature of every experience of life. By understanding the nature of waves and their characteristics, and applying that understanding to our lives, we can navigate life with a little more grace.
—Jeffrey R. Anderson, *The Nature of Things: Navigating Everyday Life with Grace*

Let's analyze each of these five factors and draw analogies to aid your Wavemaking efforts.

1. Wind Speed: Pledge Your Allegiance to God and Follow His Inspiration

At its roots, the word *inspiration* means "immediate influence of God." The essential meaning from the Greek is **"God-breathed"** or **"God-blown."** One definition in Webster's 1836 Dictionary reads: "The infusion of ideas into the mind by the Holy Spirit; the conveying into the minds of men, ideas, notices or monitions by extraordinary or supernatural influence; or the communication of the divine will to the understanding by suggestions or impressions on the mind."

Just as waves are caused by wind, your Wavemaking efforts should be inspired and influenced by God, or "God-blown." As you allow Him to "blow" the ship of your life, He can take you to destinations you cannot arrive at on your own. He provides your North Star to help you navigate through storms. He can show you sunlight through clouds.

Through waves and clouds and storms
His power will clear your way;
Wait for his time; the darkest night
Shall end in brightest day.
—Paul Gerhardt

In the ocean of life, God is our buoyant force. No matter how strong the wind and how gigantic the waves are, we will not sink because we are anchored to Him.

—Unknown

Henry Wadsworth Longfellow's classic poem *A Psalm of Life* begins with the stanza:

Tell me not, in mournful numbers,
Life is but an empty dream! —
For the soul is dead that slumbers,
And things are not what they seem.

We can be easily deceived by the glittering attractions of this world. Fame and fortune can be so alluring that our judgment is clouded in their pursuit. We think that to make a difference, we have to have celebrity status.

But throughout the ages, God has always used humble servants to do His work. Remember the story in 1 Samuel chapter 16 of the Bible, where the prophet Samuel has been called to find a new king in Israel after the Lord rejected Saul. Jesse brings his sons before Samuel to be considered for king. When Samuel sees the oldest, Eliab, he is impressed with how he looks, thinking for sure he would make a great king. But the Lord tells Samuel, in verse 7 (KJV), "Look not on his countenance, or on the height of his stature; because I have refused him: for the Lord seeth not as man seeth; for man looketh on the outward appearance, but the Lord looketh on the heart."

Being a Wavemaker is an act of faith because you don't know what impact your actions will have. With a firm allegiance to God, you can have confidence in your seem-ingly insignificant actions. Your job is to live worthy of His influence and follow His guidance in your life. You can trust that He will magnify your efforts.

> But God hath chosen the foolish things of the world to confound
> the wise; and God hath chosen the weak things of the world to
> confound the things which are mighty.
> —1 Corinthians 1:27 (KJV)

Ultimately, your *sub*mission to God is more important than your mission, for it is precisely your submission that determines your mission.

It's unclear whether all the Wavemakers featured in this book have pledged their allegiance to God. However, the point remains that doing so will magnify your efforts. The greatest Wavemakers throughout history (Mother Teresa, Martin Luther King Jr., Winston Churchill, George Washington, Benjamin Franklin, Marcus Aurelius, etc.) have all had a firm allegiance to and a humble reliance upon God.

> Self-indulgence stays in safe harbor. Obedience always leaves
> self behind and sails out in faith....Waves present opportunity!
> —Unknown

To be an effective Wavemaker, submit to God. Get your marching orders from Him. Pray to Him frequently and consistently. Ask Him to show you His will in your life. Follow the spiritual promptings you receive without hesi-tation, regardless of whether you understand the reasons why. Hold on to your faith through hard times, and trust that He is in control.

> *God sometimes delays his help to test our faith and energize our prayers. Our boat may be tossed by the waves while He sleeps but He wakes up before it sinks.*
> —Nishan Panwar

Edward Gibbon wrote, "The winds and the waves are always on the side of the ablest navigators." And the ablest navigators are those who allow God to steer their ship.

2. Fetch: Increase Your Reach and Influence by Leveraging Media

Almost all the Wavemakers featured in this book were and are masters of leveraging the media to tell their story and increase their *fetch*, or their reach and influence. Sir Sidney Smith used media by dropping leaflets into French trenches. Jonathan Edwards published numerous books. Maria Montessori traveled and gave speeches all over the world. Billy Mitchell hounded the military with a relentless and masterful media campaign. Ralph Nader routinely uses media to sway public opinion. Edward Snowden's waves have been made entirely through the media.

Here are specific ways that you can use today's media outlets to spread your message and increase your reach and influence:

- **Start a blog.** There are thousands of resources online to teach you how to do this. There are numerous free options, including Wordpress and Blogger. The two most important keys to a successful blog are (1) publish original, insightful, valuable content that really engages people and makes them want to share, and (2) publish consistently. Don't just rehash other people's content; be a true thought leader.

- **Leverage social media.** This can include Facebook, Twitter, LinkedIn, Pinterest, and other platforms. The important thing here is not to be self-indulgent, as is typical on social media. Don't just talk about yourself; really create value for the people you engage with by sharing important content. Don't bore people with trivial posts; build meaningful relationships.
- **Build an e-mail list.** This can easily be done using software such as MailChimp, AWeber, iContact, etc. Integrate this into your blog so that blog readers can subscribe to get more content from you. Publish an e-mail newsletter on a consistent basis (weekly, monthly, etc.). This also gives you an audience that can be contacted for more specific actions if an opportunity arises.
- **Publish an e-book.** Offer it on Amazon in the Kindle store. Offer a PDF version as a free gift to blog visitors who subscribe to your mailing list. Post it on social media.

Define What You Stand For and What You Stand Against

Before you can effectively leverage media, you have to define who you are, what your mission is, what you stand for, and what you stand against. The more clearly you define these things for your audience, the more inclined they will be to engage with you, and the more you attract followers who share your passion.

What you stand for are the waves you want to make. What you stand against are the waves you want to stand firm against.

Be like the cliff against which the waves continually break; but it stands firm and tames the fury of the water around it.

—Marcus Aurelius

Wavemakers are defined by what they stand against as much as by what they stand for. Sir Sidney Smith changed the world by standing against Napoleon's tyranny. Jonathan Edwards stood firm against sin and mediocrity. Maria Montessori confronted traditional teaching methods as much as she created new ones. Ralph Nader stands against corporate greed and government abuse. Edward Snowden stands against an overreaching state.

We all stand for good things. What truly defines each of us is what we stand against. What are you willing to sacrifice for? What are you willing to fight and die for?

If a man hasn't discovered something that he will die for, he isn't fit to live.

—Martin Luther King Jr.

3. Fetch Width: Develop Your Leadership Skills

One person promoting a cause makes for a narrow fetch width. To increase the width of your wave, you need to build an army of people in the trenches of your cause.

There's a big difference between being a lone maverick and a legitimate leader. We talk about "the power of one" and use people like Gandhi as an example. But never forget that without his millions of followers, Gandhi would have had very little impact. Yes, one person can make a profound difference—but that difference can't be made alone.

It is not one man nor a million, but the spirit of liberty that must be preserved. The waves which dash upon the shore are, one by one, broken, but the ocean conquers nevertheless. It overwhelms the Armada, it wears out the rock. In like manner, whatever the struggle of individuals, the great cause will gather strength.
—Lord Byron

Ralph Nader was a lone voice in the wilderness until he recruited hundreds of students to join the cause and further the work. Sir Sidney Smith could not have defeated French troops alone. If you've done your job well as a Wavemaking leader, it is the leaders you develop who will make your waves bigger and push them farther than you ever could have alone.

Aspiring Wavemakers are constantly honing their leadership skills. They submit to the mentorship of other leaders. They study great leaders from history. They constantly fill their minds with uplifting, inspiring information. They keep score and analyze their results. They learn how to build up other people.

> *Be noble! and the nobleness that lies / In other men, sleeping but never dead, / Will rise in majesty to meet thine own.*
> —James Russell Lowell

And remember, it's not about building an army of followers but rather a squadron of leaders, as Orrin Woodward and Chris Brady teach in their book *Launching a Leadership Revolution*. One person can make a splash, but a group of leaders can make tidal waves.

The aspiring Wavemaker, therefore, must be an avid student of leadership. Specifically, this means cultivating the following practices, disciplines, and habits:

- **Self-discipline.** You can't lead others if you can't lead yourself. Integrity and character are key to leadership, and their foundation is self-discipline.
- **Reading.** As the common saying goes, "Readers are leaders, and leaders are readers." Aspiring Wavemakers should read a minimum of one book per month and preferably one book per week.
- **Mentoring.** Find someone who has been where you want to go, and submit to his or her mentorship.
- **Time and energy management.** You must learn to leverage your time and energy to maximize your productivity.
- **Communication skills development.** Leaders must articulate a clear and compelling vision and must also know how to effectively motivate people.

Have you considered that if you don't make waves, nobody,
including yourself, will know that you are alive?
—Theodore Isaac Rubin

Find Something That Needs Fixing and Take Initiative to Fix It

There are things that anger you about society. That anger provides a clue to your mission. Don't just sit on your couch complaining. Get up and do something about it. As Michael Strong wrote in *Be the Solution: How Entrepreneurs and Conscious Capitalists Can Solve All the World's Problems*:

> We welcome dissatisfaction as the source of craving for the good. But we never accept whining or criticizing of others or critiques of society.
>
> If you don't like it, go fix it; go create a world, a community, a subculture in which your ideals can be instantiated, realized, in which you can show us what your vision of beauty and nobility looks like.
>
> Create a new social reality, so that I can see your dreams come true. I want to see a world in which billions of dreams are coming true constantly.
>
> ***Criticize by creating*** [emphasis added].

Billy Mitchell didn't just complain that the military wasn't taking aviation seriously enough. He gave his life and his career to the cause. Maria Montessori didn't just whine that the mentally handicapped children she met weren't being taken care of. She stepped up and did something about it.

All the world cries, "Where is the man who will save us? We want a
man!" Don't look so far for this man. You have him at hand.
This man, —it is you, it is I, it is each one of us!
—Alexandre Dumas

Noticing injustice is important. It demonstrates a consciousness that many people, who are just going through the default motions of life, don't have. But noticing is just the first step. The more important step is taking action.

Don't wait for someone else to act. Don't wait for someone to tell you what to do. Step up to the plate, stick your neck out, and lead.

Blessed is the person who sees the need, recognizes the
responsibility, and actively becomes the answer.
—William Arthur Ward

Define Success

When you act, don't do so blindly. Define exactly what you are trying to make happen and how you will measure success. In basketball, points are scored every time the ball goes through the hoop. In your efforts to make a difference, how are points scored? How do you know when you've made a difference? What concrete factors are you measuring to gauge your effectiveness or lack thereof?

It may seem redundant to say, but the people who accomplish the most in life are those who know what they want to accomplish.

I can teach anybody how to get what they want out of life. The problem is that I can't find anybody who can tell me what they want.
—Mark Twain

Every one of our featured Wavemakers had a very clearly defined goal. They all knew exactly what they were trying to make happen. And they knew exactly how they would measure success. Do you?

4. Time Duration of Wind: Perseverance

What sets Wavemakers in the arena apart from whiners on the sidelines is their willingness to commit to a cause, come what may. Wavemakers pick a mountain they're willing to die on. They plant their flag and refuse to budge or compromise.

Commitment means that it is possible for a man to yield the nerve center of his consent to a purpose or a cause, a movement or an ideal, which may be more important to him than whether he lives or dies.
—Howard Thurman

In fact, many of the greatest Wavemakers in history *have* died on their mountains. Joan of Arc was burned at the stake. Gandhi and Martin Luther King Jr. were assassinated. American colonist and Revolutionary War hero Nathan Hale proclaimed, "I only regret that I have but one life to give for my country," before being hanged by the British. Socrates, the "gadfly of the state," was found guilty of corrupting the minds of the youth of Athens and of not believing in the gods of the state and was forced to drink poison.

Consider this poem entitled "The Will to Win" by Berton Braley:

If you want a thing bad enough
To go out and fight for it,
Work day and night for it,
Give up your time and your peace and your
    sleep for it,
If only desire of it
Makes you quite mad enough
Never to tire of it,
Makes you hold all other things tawdry and
    cheap for it,
If life seems all empty and useless without it
And all that you scheme and you dream is
    about it,
If gladly you'll sweat for it,
Fret for it,
Plan for it,
Lose all your terror of God or man for it,
If you'll simply go after that thing that you want
With all your capacity,
Strength, and sagacity,
Faith, hope, and confidence, stern pertinacity,
If neither cold poverty, famished and gaunt,

Nor sickness nor pain
Of body and brain
Can turn you away from the thing that you want,
If dogged and grim you besiege and beset it,
You'll get it.

Commitment is a defining characteristic of Wavemakers. While everyone else is either jeering or cheering from the sidelines, Wavemakers are striving and sweating in the arena. While everyone else is pointing fingers, Wavemakers are digging in trenches.

The characteristic of a genuine heroism is its persistency. All men have wandering impulses, fits and starts of generosity. But when you have resolved to be great, abide by yourself, and do not weakly try to reconcile yourself with the world. The heroic cannot be the common, nor the common the heroic.
—Ralph Waldo Emerson

The greater your cause, the bigger your goal, the more time it will take to achieve. You may need to change your strategies and tactics along the way, but never give up on your objective. Keep your eye fixed upon your North Star. Pick yourself up each time you fall.

As Winston Churchill said, "Never give in—never, never, never, never, in nothing great or small, large or petty, never give in except to convictions of honour and good sense. Never yield to force; never yield to the apparently overwhelming might of the enemy."

Understand the Power of Precession

As you persevere in pursuing your goals, keep your eyes open for ripples that will appear in ways and in places that you didn't expect. Always keep in mind Buckminster Fuller's principle of "precession" ("the effect of bodies in motion on other bodies in motion"), as explained in chapter three.

When you drop a stone in water, the direct, processional movement is the stone dropping straight down to the bottom. The indirect, precessional effect is the water ripples moving outward across the surface.

It is often the same for us. We set direct goals and go to work, not understanding that it is not the goal that is important but rather what precessional effects emerge from our pursuit of the goal.

Having said that, this is precisely why it is critical to set and achieve goals. The idea is to constantly stay in motion. Without a clear purpose and a worthy pursuit of that purpose, precessional doors are never opened.

Two things to learn from this principle:

1. Set clearly defined goals, and pursue them with absolute commitment.
2. Always be alert for precessional opportunities that arise in your pursuit of your direct goals.

Before he was a Revolutionary War general, George Washington, as a youth, was a surveyor. While working in that job he gained an intimate knowledge of the terrain that he would later fight in. Thanks to his pursuit of a direct goal as a youth, he achieved a precessional objective that was far more important than being a surveyor.

Had Maria Montessori not become a doctor, she never would have served in the institution for mentally hand-icapped children. Had she not met those children, she never would have developed her methods of education. Her commitment to the direct goal of becoming a doctor opened the precessional door of her ultimate life mission.

Edward Kimble only had in mind the direct goal of converting a humble shoe salesman. Little did he under-stand the long-term precessional effects of that goal, leading up to the conversion of Billy Graham and beyond.

In your efforts to make waves, always be scanning the horizon for the precessional ripples of your direct actions, which appear only as you persevere.

Why go into something to test the waters?
Go into it and make waves.
—Anonymous

5. Water Depth: Lifelong Education and Constant Self-Improvement

The biggest ocean waves come from tsunamis, which are caused by underwater earthquakes. Likewise, the people who make the biggest waves in the world are those who have done the most work underneath the surface. In other words, you have to make waves inside yourself before they will extend beyond yourself. The more energy you spend improving yourself, the greater impact you can have improving externals.

Privately fix your own heart before marching in public protest.
—Stephen Palmer

Thus, lifelong education is key to Wavemaking. Note that almost without exception, each of the seven Wavemakers featured in this book acquired a world-class liberal arts education. Sir Sidney Smith was educated at an elite private liberal arts school. Jonathan Edwards began attending Yale at age thirteen. Maria Montessori studied at private technical schools. Billy Mitchell was educated in the classics at Columbian College of George Washington University. As a youth, Ralph Nader attended Gilbert School, a private school with the mission of "improvement of mankind by affording such assistance and means of educating the young as will help them to become good citizens," and then went on to graduate from Princeton University.

In his fabulous book *A Thomas Jefferson Education: Teaching a Generation of Leaders for the Twenty-First Century*, Oliver DeMille details how you can earn a world-class leadership education throughout your life, no matter your previous educational background. The fundamental component of a leadership education is studying the greatest classics in history, which convey the greatest ideas taught by the greatest minds. "As students become familiar with and eventually conversant with the great ideas of humanity," Oliver teaches, "they learn how to think, how to lead, and how to become great."[6]

It is chiefly through books that we enjoy intercourse with superior minds....In the best books, great men [and women] talk to us, give us their most precious thoughts, and pour their souls into ours.
—William Ellery Channing

Author Roy H. Williams writes, "A smart man makes a mistake, learns from it, and never makes that mistake again. But a wise man finds a smart man and learns from him how to avoid the mistake altogether." Classics give us virtually unlimited smart men and women to learn from. By reading, we can learn from the mistakes of others and get ideas from their successes.

You can't stop the waves, but you can learn to surf.
—Jon Kabat-Zinn

In addition, as Oliver DeMille writes:

Knowledge of human nature is the key to leadership...the thing which makes a classic great is glaring insight into basic human nature. Ultimately, as you study the classics, you learn about your own personal nature. Learning through experience is good, but it is often better to learn from someone else's experiences and build on them—we hope a baby will learn from his parents not to touch a hot stove, even though the actual experience would certainly have impact. If we will let them, the classics can teach us lessons without the pain of repeating certain mistakes ourselves. They can show us correct choices which will get us where we want to go....

Classics allow us to experience, in an intimate way, the greatest mistakes and successful choices of human history. If we learn from these mistakes and successes, we will make fewer mistakes and have more successes.

At a deeper level, knowing how others think, feel and act allows us to predict behavior and act accordingly. We can develop empathy, compassion, wisdom, and self-discipline without subjecting our relationships to a more painful learning curve. This is invaluable to the entrepreneur, parent, community leader or statesman. People with experience have been through certain patterns many times and know what to anticipate. The classics can provide us with many such experiences.

Of course, it's not enough to simply educate ourselves; we must constantly be striving to actually improve ourselves. In other words, it's not just about learning so we can achieve objectives. It's about becoming a better person, a better servant, a better leader. In short, true education is not about technical knowledge but rather about becoming great.

Jonathan Edwards is an excellent role model in this regard. We can learn from his personal resolutions to set resolutions for ourselves and hold ourselves accountable to them. This requires honest self-appraisal. Aspiring Wavemakers can never be content to rest on their laurels.

They must always be asking themselves where they've fallen short and where they need to improve to become more effective leaders.

The important thing is this: to be able at any moment to sacrifice what we are for what we could become.
—Charles Dubois

William Shakespeare wrote, "Like as the waves make towards the pebbl'd shore, so do our minutes hasten to their end." Life is too short to spend it splashing around in the kiddie pool of selfishness and mediocrity. You were born for a purpose. You were born for greatness. You were born to make waves and leave a legacy.

Never waste a minute or a fraction of your precious energy on trivial pursuits. Engage in a great cause that is worthy of your heritage as a child of God. Follow Gandhi's advice to "Be the change you wish to see in the world." Make a difference. Be somebody worth remembering.

There's a great, wide ocean out there that needs your unique gifts, talents, and passions. Now set sail and go make some waves....

Introduction

1   Stephen Palmer, Uncommon Sense: A Common Citizen's Guide to Rebuilding America (The Center for Social Leadership, 2010).

2   Roy H. Williams, "The Four People You Meet on the Ocean of Life," *http://mondaymorningmemo.com/newsletters/read/1686*.

Chapter One

1   Tom Pocock, *A Thirst for Glory: The Life of Admiral Sir Sidney Smith* (London: Thistle Publishing, 2013).

2   Ibid.

3   Ibid.

4   Ibid.

5   Ibid.

6   Chris Brady, *Rascal: Making a Difference by Becoming an Original Character* (Flint, MI: Obstaclés Press, 2010).

7   Pocock, *A Thirst for Glory*.

8   Ibid.

9   Ibid.

10   Ibid.

11   Ibid.

12   Ibid.

13   Ibid.

14   Ibid.

15   Ibid.

16   Ibid.

17   Ibid.

18   Ibid.

19   Edward Howard, *The Memoirs of Sir Sidney Smith* (Tucson, AZ: Fireship Press, 2007).

20   Pocock, *A Thirst for Glory*.

21   Ibid.

22   Ibid.

23   Howard, *The Memoirs of Sir Sidney Smith*.

24   Pocock, *A Thirst for Glory*.

25   Ibid.

26   Ibid.

27   Ibid.

28   Ibid.

29   Ibid.

30   Robert Kiyosaki, *Rich Dad, Poor Dad: What the Rich Teach Their Kids about Money That the Poor and Middle Class Do Not!* (New York: Warner Books, 1997).

31   Pocock, *A Thirst for Glory*.

32   Ibid.

33   Ibid.

Chapter Two

1   Richard L. Dugdale, *The Jukes: A Study in Crime, Pauperism, Disease, and Heridity* (New York: The Knickerbocker Press, 1877).

2   Albert Edward Winship, *Jukes-Edwards: A Study in Education and Heredity* (Charleston, SC: Nabu Press, 2010).

3   Ibid.

4   Ibid.

5   Wikipedia,http://en.wikipedia.org/wiki/ Jonathan_Edwards_(theologian)

6   George M. Marsden, *Jonathan Edwards: A Life* (New Haven, CT: Yale University Press, 2004).

7   Ibid.

8   Ibid.

9   Ibid.

10   *The Works of Jonathan Edwards*, Volume One (New Haven, CT: Yale University Press, 2009).

11   Orrin Woodward, *RESOLVED: 13 Resolutions for LIFE* (Flint, MI: Obstaclés Press, 2012).

12   Marsden, *Jonathan Edwards: A Life*.

13   Ibid.

14   Ibid.

15   Ibid.

16   Ibid.

17   Ibid.

18   Ibid.

19   Ibid.

20   Ibid.

21   Ibid.

22   Ibid.

23   Ibid.

24   Ibid.

25   Ibid.

26   Ibid.

27   Marsden, *Jonathan Edwards: A Life*.

28   Ibid.

29   Ibid.

30   Ibid.

31   Ibid.

32   Ibid.

33   Winship, *Jukes-Edwards*.

34   Ibid.

35   Ibid.

Chapter Three

1   Rita Kramer, *Maria Montessori: A Biography* (Chicago, University of Chicago Press, 1976).

2   Ibid.

3   Ibid.

4   E. M. Standing, *Maria Montessori: Her Life and Work* (New York: Plume, 1998).

5   Henry Wadsworth Longfello, "The Ladder of St. Augustine," *The Courtship of Miles Standish and Other Poems* (1858).

6   Standing, *Maria Montessori: Her Life and Work*.

7   Kramer, *Maria Montessori: A Biography*.

8   Ibid.

9   Standing, *Maria Montessori: Her Life and Work*.

10   Ibid.

11   Ibid.

12   Ibid.

13   Ibid.

14   Ibid.

15   Ibid.

16   Kramer, *Maria Montessori: A Biography*.

17   Chris Brady, *A Month of Italy: Rediscovering the Art of Vacation* (Flint, MI: Obstaclés Press, 2012).

18   Stephen Covey, "*The 7 Habits of Highly Effective People*: Habit 7: Sharpen the Saw," https://www.stephencovey.com/7habits/7habits-habit7.php.

19   Kramer, *Maria Montessori: A Biography*.

20   Standing, *Maria Montessori: Her Life and Work*.

21   Ibid.

22   Montessori, Maria, *The Secret of Childhood* (New York: Ballantine Books, 1982).

23   Kramer, *Maria Montessori: A Biography*.

24   Ibid.

25   Ibid.

26   Ibid.

27   Ibid.

28   Ibid.

29   Ibid.

30   Ibid.

31   Standing, *Maria Montessori: Her Life and Work*.

32   Ibid.

33   Kramer, *Maria Montessori: A Biography*.

34   Ibid.

35   Chris Brady and Orrin Woodward, *Launching a Leadership Revolution* (Flint, MI: Obstaclés Press, 2012).

36   Standing, *Maria Montessori: Her Life and Work*.

37   Kramer, *Maria Montessori: A Biography*.

38   "How Many Montessori Schools Are There?," copyright 2014, North American Montessori Teachers' Association (NAMTA),

http://www.montessori-namta.org/FAQ/Montessori-Education/
How-many-Montessori-schools-are-there.

39   Standing, *Maria Montessori: Her Life and Work*.

Chapter Four

1   Alfred F. Hurley, *Billy Mitchell: Crusader for Air Power*
(Bloomington, IN: Indiana University Press, 2006).

2   Ibid.

3   Ibid.

4   Ibid.

5   Ibid.

6   Ibid.

7   Ibid.

8   Ibid.

9   Ibid.

10   Ibid.

11   Ibid.

12   Ibid.

13   Ibid.

14   Ibid.

15   Ibid.

16   Ibid.

17   Ibid.

18   Ibid.

19   Ibid.

20   Ibid.

21   Ibid.

22   Ibid.

23   Ibid.

24   Ibid.

25   Douglas Waller, *A Question of Loyalty: General Billy
Mitchell and the Court-Martial That Gripped the Nation* (New York:
HarperCollins, 2004).

26   Ibid.

27   Ibid.

28   http://en.wikipedia.org/wiki/Billy_Mitchell

29   Ibid.

30   Hurley, *Billy Mitchell: Crusader for Air Power*.
31   Waller, *A Question of Loyalty*.
32   Ibid.
33   Ibid.

Chapter Five

1   Troy Anderson, "Billy Graham to Give 'Final, Most Important' Message," World Net Daily, November 6, 2012, http://www.wnd.com/2013/11/billy-graham-to-give-final-most-important-message/.

2   My Hope America with Billy Graham, "The Cross," copyright 2014 Billy Graham Evangelistic Association, http://myhopewithbillygraham.org/programs/the-cross/.

3   "Biography of Billy Graham," copyright 2014 Billy Graham Evangelistic Association, billygraham.org/about/biographies/billy-graham/.

4   Anderson, "Billy Graham to Give 'Final, Most Important' Message."

5   Sword of the Lord "Preacher Biographies," copyright 1934-2014 Sword of the Lord, http://www.swordofthelord.com/biographies.php.

6   Ibid.

7   Berean Internet Ministry, "D. L. Moody's Salvation," http://www.bereaninternetministry.org/D.%20L.%20Moody%27s%20Testimony.htm, accessed March 25, 2014.

8   Sword of the Lord "Preacher Biographies."

9   Believersweb, "Biography of John Wilbur Chapman," posted March 13, 2003, http://www.believersweb.org/view.cfm?ID=116.

10   Ibid.

11   Ibid.

12   Wikimedia, "Billy Sunday," last modified March 21, 2014 at 03:55, Wikimedia Foundation Inc., http://en.wikipedia.org/wiki/Billy_Sunday.

13   Ibid.

14   Sword of the Lord "Preacher Biographies."

15   Ibid.

16   Ibid.

Chapter Six

1   Ralph Nader, *The Seventeen Traditions* (New York: Harper, 2007).

2   Ibid.

3   Ibid.

4   Patricia Cronin Marcello, *Ralph Nader: A Biography* (Westport, CT: Greenwood Press, 2004).

5   Ibid.

6   Nader, *The Seventeen Traditions*.

7   Ibid.

8   Ibid.

9   Ibid.

10   Marcello, *Ralph Nader: A Biography*.

11   Nader, *The Seventeen Traditions*.

12   Ibid.

13   Ibid.

14   Ibid.

15   Marcello, *Ralph Nader: A Biography*.

16   Ibid.

17   Ibid.

18   Ibid.

19   Ibid.

20   Ibid.

21   Ibid.

22   Ralph de Toledano, *Hit and Run: The Rise – and Fall? – of Ralph Nader* (Rochelle, NY: Arlington House, 1975).

23   Marcello, *Ralph Nader: A Biography*.

24   Ibid.

25   Ibid.

26   Ibid.

27   Ibid.

28   Ibid.

29   Ibid.

30   Ibid.

31   Ibid.

Chapter Seven

1   Meenal Vamburkar, "Edward Snowden's Father Speaks Out to Fox About Media's 'Misinformation,' Asks Son to Stop Leaking," *Mediaite*, June 17, 2013, http://www.mediaite.com/tv/edward-snowdens-father-speaks-out-to-fox-about-media-misinformation-asks-son-to-stop-leaking/.

2   John M. Broder and Scott Shane, "For Snowden, a Life of Ambition, Despite the Drifting," *The New York Times*, June 15, 2013.

3   Ibid.

4   Glenn Greenwald, "Edward Snowden: The Whistleblower Behind the NSA Surveillance Revelations," *The Guardian*, June 9, 2013.

5   Broder and Shane, "For Snowden, a Life of Ambition, Despite the Drifting."

6   Greenwald, "Edward Snowden: The Whistleblower Behind the NSA Surveillance Revelations."

7   Ibid.

8   Lana Lam, "Snowden Sought Booz Allen Job to Gather Evidence on NSA Surveillance," *South China Morning Post Hong Kong*, June 24, 2013.

9   Andy Greenberg, "An NSA Coworker Remembers the Real Edward Snowden: 'A Genius Among Geniuses'", *Forbes Magazine*, December 16, 2013, http://www.forbes.com/sites/andygreenberg/2013/12/16/an-nsa-coworker-remembers-the-real-edward-snowden-a-genius-among-geniuses/.

10   Gabriel Rodriquez, "Edward Snowden Interview Transcript," *PolicyMic*, June 9, 2013.

11   Barton Gellman, "Code Name 'Verax': Snowden, in Exchanges with Post Reporters, Made Clear He Knew Risks," *The Washington Post*, June 9, 2013.

12   Shashank Bengali and Ken Dilanian, "Edward Snowden Vows More Disclosures about U.S. Surveillance," *The Los Angeles Times*, June 17, 2013.

13   Greenwald, "Edward Snowden: The Whistleblower Behind the NSA Surveillance Revelations."

14   Bengali and Dilanian, "Edward Snowden Vows More Disclosures About U.S. Surveillance."

15   Rodriquez, "Edward Snowden Interview Transcript."

16   Peter Finn and Sari Horwitz, "U.S. Charges Snowden with Espionage," *The Washington Post*, June 21, 2013.

17   Shasta Darlington and Catherine E. Shoichet, "Brazil, Mexico Summon U.S. Ambassadors over Espionage Reports," CNN. com, September 3, 2013.

18   Josh Levs, "Snowden's Open Letter Offers to Help Brazil Investigate NSA Surveillance," CNN.com, December 18, 2013.

19   Glenn Greenwald, "NSA Collecting Phone Records of Millions of Verizon Customers Daily," *The Guardian*, June 5, 2013.

20   "Latest Snowden Leak Reveals NSA's Goal to Continually Expand Surveillance Abilities," RT.com, November 23, 2013.

21   Greenwald, "Edward Snowden: The Whistleblower Behind the NSA Surveillance Revelations."

22   Barton Gellman, "Behind the Interview: How Snowden Thinks," *Washington Post* Video, http://www.washingtonpost. com/posttv/national/behind-the-interview-how-snowden-thinks/2013/12/24/40881f74-6cde-11e3-b405-7e360f7e9fd2_video. html.

23   Rodriquez, "Edward Snowden Interview Transcript."

24   Barton Gellman, "Edward Snowden, after Months of NSA Revelations, Says His Mission's Accomplished," *The Washington Post*, December 23, 2013.

25   Debbie Hines, "All the Focus on Edward Snowden is Misplaced," *Huffington Post*, January 12, 2014.

Chapter Eight

1   Story quoted from Stephen Palmer, *Manifest Destiny: Choosing a Life of Greatness* (Cedar City, UT: Colesville Academy, 2013).

2   Edward Hall, *The Silent Language* (New York: Anchor Books, 1973).

3   Glenn Welker, "The Constitution of the Iroquois Nations: The Great Binding Law Gayanashagowa," copyright 1993-2014, last updated February 3, 2014 19:08:05, http://www.indigenouspeople. net/iroqcon.htm.

4   Wikipedia, "Seven Generation Sustainability," Wikimedia Foundation Inc., last modified December 7, 2013 at 07:45, http://en.wikipedia.org/wiki/Seven_generation_sustainability.

5   Wikipedia, "Wave," Wikimedia Foundation Inc., last modified March 22, 2014 at 14:03, http://en.wikipedia.org/wiki/Wave.

6   Oliver DeMille, *A Thomas Jefferson Education: Teaching a Generation of Leaders for the Twenty-First Century* (Cedar City, UT: George Wythe College Press, 2006).

Other Books in the LIFE Leadership Essentials Series

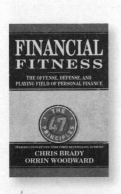

Financial Fitness: The Offense, Defense, and Playing Field of Personal Finance **with Introduction by Chris Brady and Orrin Woodward – $21.95**
If you ever feel that you're too far behind and can't envision a better financial picture, you are so WRONG! You need this book! The *Financial Fitness* book is for everyone at any level of wealth. Just like becoming physically or mentally fit, becoming financially fit requires two things: knowing what to do and taking the necessary action to do it. Learn how to prosper, conserve, and become fiscally fantastic. It's a money thing, and the power to prosper is all yours!

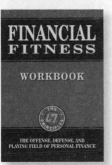

Financial Fitness Workbook **– $7.95**
Economic affairs don't have to be boring or stressful. Make managing money fun in a few simple steps. Use this workbook to get off to a great start and then continue down the right path to becoming fiscally fabulous! Discover exactly where all of your money actually goes as you make note of all your expenditures. Every page will put you one step closer to financial freedom, so purchase the *Financial Fitness Workbook* today and get budgeting!

Mentoring Matters: Targets, Techniques, and Tools for Becoming a Great Mentor **with Foreword by Orrin Woodward – $19.95**
Get your sticky notes ready for all the info you're about to take in from this book. Do you know what it means to be a *great* mentor? It's a key part of successful leadership, but for most people, the necessary skills and techniques don't come naturally. Educate yourself on all of the key targets, techniques, and tools for becoming a magnificent mentor with this easy-to-apply manual. Your leadership success will be forever increased!

Turn the Page: How to Read Like a Top Leader with Introduction by Chris Brady – $15.95

Leaders are readers. But there are many ways to read, and leaders read differently than most people do. They read to learn what they need to know, do, or feel, regardless of the author's intent or words. They see past the words and read with the specific intent of finding truth and applying it directly in their own lives. Learn how to read like a top leader so you'll be better able to emulate their success. Applying the skills taught in *Turn the Page* will impact your life, career, and leadership abilities in ways you can't even imagine. So turn the page and start reading!

SPLASH!: A Leader's Guide to Effective Public Speaking with Foreword by Chris Brady – $15.95

For many, the fear of giving a speech is worse than the fear of death. But public speaking can be truly enjoyable *and* a powerful tool for making a difference in the lives of others. Whether you are a beginner or a seasoned orator, this book will help you transform your public speaking to a whole new level of leadership influence. Learn the SPLASH formula for great public speaking that will make you the kind of speaker and leader who makes a SPLASH—leaving any audience, big or small, forever changed—every time you speak!

The Serious Power of Fun with Foreword by Chris Brady – $15.95

Life got you down? Feeling like life isn't much fun is a bad place to be. Fun matters. It is serious business and a source of significant leadership power. Without it, few people maintain the levels of inspired motivation and sustained effort that bring great success. So put a smile back on your face. Discover how to make every area of life more enjoyable and turn any situation into the right kind of fun. Learn to cultivate a habit of designed gratification—where life just keeps getting better—and *laugh your way to increased success* with *The Serious Power of Fun!*

Subscriptions and Products from
LIFE Leadership

Rascal Radio Subscription – $49.95 per month
Rascal Radio by LIFE Leadership is the world's first online personal development radio hot spot. Rascal Radio is centered on LIFE Leadership's 8 Fs: Faith, Family, Finances, Fitness, Following, Freedom, Friends, and Fun. Subscribers have unlimited access to **hundreds and hundreds** of audio recordings that they can stream endlessly from both the LIFE Leadership website and the **LIFE Leadership Smartphone App.** Listen to one of the preset stations or customize your own based on speaker or subject. Of course, you can easily skip tracks or "like" as many as you want. And if you are listening from the website, you can purchase any one of these incredible audios.

Let Rascal Radio provide you with **life-changing information to help you live the life you've always wanted!**

The LIFE Series – $50.00 per month
Here's where LIFE Leadership began—with the now famously followed 8 Fs: Family, Finances, Fitness, Faith, Following, Freedom, Friends, and Fun. This highly recommended series offers a strong foundation on which to build and advance in every area of your daily life. The timeless truths and effective strategies included will reignite passion and inspire you to be your very best. Transform your life for the better and watch how it will create positive change in the lives of those around you. Subscribe today and have the time of your LIFE!

Series includes 4 audios and 1 book monthly and is also available in Spanish and French.

The LLR (Launching a Leadership Revolution) Series – $50.00 per month

There is no such thing as a born leader. Based on the *New York Times* bestseller *Launching a Leadership Revolution* by Chris Brady and Orrin Woodward, this series focuses on teaching leadership skills at every level. The principles and specifics taught in the LLR Series will equip you with all the tools you need for business advancement, community influence, church impact, and even an advantage in your home life. Topics include: leadership, finances, public speaking, goal setting, mentoring, game planning, accountability and tracking of progress, levels of motivation and influence, and leaving a personal legacy. Will you be ready to take the lead when you're called? Subscribe now and learn how to achieve effective confidence skills while growing stronger in your leadership ability.

Series includes 4 audios and 1 leadership book monthly.

The AGO (All Grace Outreach) Series – $25.00 per month

We are all here together to love one another and take care of each other. But sometimes in this hectic world, we lose our way and forget our true purpose. When you subscribe to the AGO Series, you'll gain the valuable support and guidance that every Christian searches for. Nurture your soul, strengthen your faith, and find answers to better understand God's plan for your life, marriage, and children.

Series includes 1 audio and 1 book monthly.

The Edge Series – $10.00 per month

You'll cut in front of the rest of the crowd when you get the *Edge*. Designed for those on the younger side of life, this hard-core, no-frills series promotes self-confidence, drive, and motivation. Get advice, timely information, and true stories of success from interesting talks and fascinating people. Block out the noise around you and learn the principles of self-improvement at an early age. It's a gift that will keep on giving from parent to child. Subscribe today and get a competitive *Edge* on tomorrow.

Series includes 1 audio monthly.

The Freedom Series – $10.00 per month
Freedom must be fought for if it is to be preserved. Every nation and generation needs people who are willing to take a stand for it. Are you one of those brave leaders who'll answer the call? Gain an even greater understanding of the significance and power of freedom, get better informed on issues that affect yours, and find out how you can prevent its decline.

This series covers freedom matters that are important to *you*. Make your freedom and liberty a priority and subscribe today.

Series includes 1 audio monthly.

Financial Fitness Subscription – $10.00 per month for 12 months
If you found the *Financial Fitness Pack* life-changing and beneficial to your bank account, then you'll want even more timely information and guidance from the Financial Fitness Subscription. It's designed as a continuing economic education to help people develop financial discipline and overall knowledge of how their money works. Learn how to make financial principles your financial habits. It's a money thing, and it always pays to be cash savvy.

Subscription includes 1 audio monthly for 12 months.

LIFE Library Subscription – $40.00 per month
You'll never be shushed in this library. This online, round-the-clock resource is the best connection to LIFE Leadership's latest and greatest leadership content. You can watch or listen in either video or audio format, and easy access allows you to search by format, speaker, or subject. Go exploring through the entire content of the LIFE Library. Subscribe today, tune in, and turn it up.

LIFE Live Subscription – $40.00 per month
Are you missing out on LIFE? LIFE Live gives you an all-access pass to LIFE Leadership Seminars or Webinars all across North America. This cost-effective subscription lets you attend live gatherings in person or by viewing a LIFE Leadership Webinar from wherever you are. The LIFE/LLR Session kicks off these live events, which can range in size from a couple hundred to thousands of participants. Now you can continue to keep up with beneficial content and get the latest information you want. Subscribe today. We look forward to seeing you LIVE!

Financial Fitness Pack **– $99.99**
Once and for all, it's time to free yourself from the worry and heavy burden of debt. Decide today to take an honest look at your finances by learning and applying the simple principles of financial success. The *Financial Fitness Pack* provides you with all the tools needed to get on a path to becoming fiscally fantastic!

 Pack includes the Financial Fitness *book, a companion workbook, and 8 audio recordings.*